from Pen (elope) with love xxx

from Pen (elope) with love
xxx

Poems and Prose by Diana Button

Poet in Residence Press

Germany, Italy, Luxembourg, United Kingdom.

Bibliographic information of the German National Library:
the German National Library (Deutsche Nationalbibliothek)
catalogs this publication in the German National Bibliography
(Deutsche Nationalbibliografie).

Detailed bibliographic information can be found
on the internet website: http://dnb.ddb.de.

Produced and published in Germany by:
BoD – Books on Demand, Norderstedt, Germany.

ISBN: 978-3-7504-1909-4

For the family of man,
this miraculous journey
and the opportunity
to wake up
together.

Acknowledgements

No book is ever the work of one person alone. Even if only one person puts pen to paper, it is always an act that happens with the support of many others whom I would like to honour here.

Thank you, Norbert, my dear husband, and Kevin and Erik, my dear sons for all your love and support. You enrich every moment of my life through your free spirits and creative hearts. A special mention to Kevin: it was your booklet, Poetry on the Move that inspired me to publish this work. Your offering reminded me how important it is to share our writing widely in the world.

Thank you, Sarah Mason, my dear friend of thirty-seven years, for walking the spiritual path with me and for our many rich, thought-provoking and heartwarming conversations along the way.

Thank you, Tricia Heriz-Smith, dear friend and sister poet for all the cross fertilisation in poetry. I am so very grateful for our many poetry exchanges over the years and that you kindly offered to proof-read my manuscript and write the foreword.

Many poems in these pages were inspired by the Poet-in-Residence group meetings at my house or in cyber space. Thank you for sharing your vulnerable poet hearts and in doing so, repeatedly encouraging me to do the same: Roland Brinkhoff, Susie Clare, Sanford Clark, Nada Kojic-Edwards, Neil Houltram, Theresa Loder, Lori McDonald, Sultana Raza, Jennifer Rundle, David Rynick, Frank Telwest, Ana Villalobos and Wendy Winn.

I am deeply grateful to many others who have supported and honoured my creativity: my mum and dad, Karen and Derrick; my sisters Corinna, Nicola and Julia; writers, friends, teachers and mentors including: Melissa Blacker, Mary Carey, Stewart Cooper, Roderick Dunnett, Sylvie Flammang, Helga Goehring-Schneider, Charles Muller, Angela Pisani, Beate Ronnefeldt, Dana Rufolo, Sophie Seale, Naomi Tasker, Susan Tiberghien, Roos Vrouwe and Martina Zähner-Scheel.

Thank you, yogis and yoginis who practice yoga with me: I feel your beautiful energy flowing in my heart and into my writing.

Please forgive me if I have not mentioned you here by name. I bow to you now and thank you from the bottom of my heart.

Contents

Acknowledgements vi
Foreword xiii
Preface.. xv

POEMS ALL THE WAY **19**
Hands.. 21
Muses of a Creative... 22
I have woken up... 23
Lion on the Sofa.. 24
A Cup of Yogi Tea.. 26
Sun Salutations... 27
Your Birthday 29
Softy.. 31
A Tea Party 32
Alchemy? 33
March.. 34
Breaking the Fast 35
Harvesting.. 36
Me and My Beanstalk 37
Queen of Middle Age 38
Soft Fruit Season... 39
What is Your Teaching, Body?.. 41
What Body Has to Say 43
Shadow and I.. 45
Wholly Human.. 46
View from a Heart 49
On Being Human 51
Love in the Lawn.. 53
Under the Waxing Moon... 55
Dream Spirit 56
Life in Prints 57
Yes and No Game.. 58
Mare Nostrum... 59
Onset of Spring... 60
Where are you going so hastily? 61
Poetry on the Lake 62
Imagine This! 64
Dear Gardener, ... 65
It's Official 66
Eavesdropping... 67
Venus and Moon Mind the Night... 68
By Water's Edge 69
Moon Meditation... 71
If Conditions 72
Dropping the Tissue... 73

Metamorphosis 75
Today I Awake 76
Coming Back 77
Under the Bodhi Tree 78
At my Open Door 79
Feeling What we are Feeling 80
Day after Day of Downpour 81
How to Joy Ride 82
Up with the Larks 83
Thoughts and I 84
Ushered In? 86
Shopping for Cheese 87
An Age, 26 89
Everywhere and Nowhere 91
I am a Weeping Woman 93
Beyond Measure 95
Sister Love 96
As you Are 97
A Taste for Mu 98
Haiku or 17-Syllable Floats? 99

POEMS ON SUNDAYS **103**
A Poem on Sunday I 105
A Poem on Sunday II 106
A Poem on Sunday III 108
A Poem on Sunday IV 109
Beside Myself 110
Some Sundays 111
Morning has Broken 112
Purple 113
I Bow to the Peach Tree 114
When you Come...When You Go 115
Winter Meditation 116
Blessed be the Face 117
Grace 119
Retreat 120
Para Doxa 121
Bless the Children 122
Blind Navigation 124
On Your Own Side 126
One Key Fits All 127
This Morning on the Rocky Ridge 128
New Year Advice I Like to Abide by 129
Memo: remember to remember 131
Instructions for a Whole Heart 132
Remember: you are 133
Choose Love? 134
Advice for a Spiritual Warrior 136

On This Path 137
Into Your Element.. 138
The Question is Not 139
Breathing Room... 140
Morning Mantras 141
Trusty Compass... 142
Here with Me 143

POEMS FOR WRITERS **145**
The Delivery Room... 147
Serious Advice for Unformed Poets.................................... 148
What to Remember Each Morning...................................... 150
Before the Poetry Reading 151
Poet in Residence.. 152
What is a Poem? 154
Poem Falls.. 156
Divine Force Shapes 158
Poetry Time.. 159
Poet in Residence Life 160
Another Writing Book 161
Usually it's a Tuesday 162
I Cannot Hold Back.. 163
Twinkle in Your Eye 164
Sometimes and Then... All is Resonance 165
Morning Writing Practice.. 167
Intent 169
I Dip In 170
No Midsummer Day's Breeze 171
Catcher of the Prose.. 173

POEMS PLAY AND SHAPE... **177**
Wish upon a Star... 179
In this Garden 180
Germitaleng I.. 181
Germitaleng II... 182
Bedtime in Luxembourg.. 183
Fouling around the Fruit Bowl 184
Strictly for the Birds 185
In the Place I am Now 186
Anticipating the Call 188
Back Together... 189
Water Borne 190
Mindful Moment 191
Dressing in Blessing 192
1: One Company 193
Wholly Communion 194

SONNETS.. **195**
   Sonnet I.. 197
   Sonnet II... 198
   Sonnet III.. 199
   Sonnet IV.. 200
   Sonnet V... 201
   Sonnet VI.. 202
   Sonnet VII... 203
   Sonnet VIII.. 204

THIS IS NOT ABOUT POEMS.. **205**
   This is not about Butterflies.. 207
   This is not about Lizards... 208
   This is not about Thunder... 209
   This is not about Leaves... 210
   This is not about Star Trek 211
   This is not about Fennel 212
   This is not about Soup.. 213
   This is not about Coffee Tables..................................... 214
   This is not about Blackbird Song 215
   This is not about Cloaks.. 216
   This is not about Engines.. 217
   This is not about Herons... 218
   This is not about Pumas.. 219
   This is not about Clocks.. 220
   This is not about Time 221
   This is not about Beaches.. 223
   This is not about Breezes.. 224
   This is not about Ladybirds.. 225
   This is not about Light... 226
   This is not about Frida Kahlo and Diego Rivera 227
   This is not about Fact, but Meaning............................... 229
   This is not about Judgement, but Truth........................... 230

AFTER POEMS **231**
   The Mind and The Heart 233
   Greed and the Big Feed... 235
   Thank You...I am: a writer's song................................... 236
   Ode to Rough Paper 238
   Sonnet XVIII 241
   There's a Wook in my Book 242

ESSAYS AND PROSE... **245**
   Under the Wisteria.. 247
   Morning Pages 249
   Shutters 251
   Timing the Growth 253
   Feeling the Well 255

Plucking Eyebrows...257
Sacre Coeur...258
Travelling to the Yoke...260
Berlinese Impressions...272
Fricassée Argenteuil...275
Man's Unsexy Wife...280
Man's Stressful Wife...283
The Doctor and his Pet Chimpanzee..................................284
Dial S-T-R-E-S-S for Success..286
The Flute Player...288
Into a Breath of Warm Air...290
She...292
Peppermint Moment..296
Horse Power..300
Enough to make a Cat Laugh..302
Dear Reader,...305

ITALIANO **307**
Andiamo in Italia 309
Regali del Passato 311
L' Estate del Duemillasette...313
Due Bambini e un Gatto 314
Il Mio Più Caro Amico 317
La Luna e L'Amore 319
I Capelli di Clara 320
La Nostra Pendola 321
L' Esame...322
La Studentessa 323
Il Vecchio Libro 324
Una Nascità Rapida 325
Danza Settimanale...327
Leone sul Divano 329

LETTERS AND POSTCARDS...**331**
Dear writer friend, ...333
Dear soul sister, ...337
Dear creative friend,...339
My dear friend, ...343
Dearest soul sister, ...345
Hello my dear, dear friend,..347
Postcard I 350
Postcard II 351
Postcard III 352
Dear Pen (elope), ...353
Postcard IV 355

AFTERWORD AND RESOURCES **357**
  About the Author: Spiritual Autobiography 359
  Poet in Residence Blog and Press 366
  Teachings and Wise Words Along the Way........................ 367
  Books by the Same Author.. 372

Foreword

What a privilege it is to be asked to write a foreword to this moving and beautiful book that Diana has created. It is testament to her incredible fortitude, courage, tenacity and humility as well as a collection of intensely moving and intimate insights into a personal journey with which we can all, in some way, identify.

from Pen (elope) with love xxx is hard to put down once you begin, yet each entry calls for its own time and space, inviting the reader to linger and savour the richness of the imagery, the depths of emotion and thought, the beacons of hope and change that it encompasses.

It is the kind of book I will revisit many times, to dip in randomly and allow Pen (elope) to stimulate my creativity from within its varied offerings: It is a lighthouse for others undertaking a similar journey of self-discovery as it explores different terrains and differing routes to arrive at that place we all seek

> We shall not cease from exploration, and the end of all our exploring will be to arrive where we started and know the place for the first time[1]

Diana, thank you for your courage in gifting us with this work of over twenty years to guide us on our personal journey.

With love,

Tricia Heriz-Smith xxx

---

[1] From Little Gidding, the last of T. S. Eliot's Four Quartets. Printed with permission from Faber and Faber Ltd. Royalty Department Burnt Mill Elizabeth Way Harlow Essex, CM20 2HX England.

Preface

> You are not
> a troubled guest
> on this earth,
> you are not
> an accident
> amidst other accidents,
> you were invited
> from another and greater
> night
> than the one
> from which
> you have just emerged.[2]

Writing is my home. I have known this for years and yet it only became a mantra during my years in Italy. Moving was an adventure with many exciting moments, both challenging and stimulating. At times, I was inspired to create and explore new territory with gusto and delight, other times, I fell victim to my innermost human vulnerability and the thought that I was, indeed, 'a troubled guest on this earth'.

During those moments, not only did I feel disconnected from the outside world, the Italian language and culture, but also from my own inner world. I felt truly lost, physically and spiritually homeless. Yet, in that seemingly impossible place, if I kept quiet and patient, my creative voice would start to softly speak to me and I would begin to write. Just forming words, making sentences, putting thoughts down on paper was enough to loosen the tight hold of the closed, rigid, or polarised mind I was caught in.

So that I do not forget that writing is my true north and trusted navigator through life, I have created this book, *from Pen (elope)*

---

[2] From the poem by David Whyte, What to Remember When Waking (The House of Belonging, 2011). Printed with permission from Many Rivers Press, www.davidwhyte.com. ©Many Rivers Press, Langley, WA USA.

with love xxx. It contains a selection of poems, prose pieces and letters from the past two decades of my life.

Through my personal journey and experience, I have learned to trust that writing has the power to bring us back to ourselves, our humanness. It can take us out of depression, despair and darkness; a sense of hopelessness, separateness or not belonging, and back in touch with the larger, all-encompassing, inter-connected beings that we are. In this way, writing can teach us how to be peaceful and wholehearted in relation to ourselves, others and all of life.

I further believe that writing (and in particular, poetry) is a mysterious messenger. We do not think poems and prose up, rather, they come to us. On fortunate days, I catch some as they float down to Earth.

Sometimes, writing comes in the form of a question; other times as a prayer or blessing. Sometimes, writing points to where I need to pay urgent attention; other times it brings important insights about who I am - who we are.

The title *from Pen (elope) with love xxx* is meant to hint at the intimate and personal nature of the work. It is, of course, how you might end a letter or message to someone near and dear to you. Despite some of the challenging ground covered as I explore many aspects of being human with its emotional messiness and difficulty, the title also hints at the playfulness, humour, and moments of childlike wonder that are also very much present in the work.

Indeed, you may have already noticed the playfulness in the way Pen (elope) is written, how it is made up of the words *pen* and *elope*.

Pen (elope) is the name I give my inner writer – the one who cares about me and the importance of creative writing in my life. She offers kind, but constructive criticism, and has accompanied me over the years. I consider her my muse, soul mate; as faithful and trustworthy as any a friend I have in the outer world.

Though I primarily chose the name Pen(elope) because it contains the word *pen*. I also like how the meaning of *elope* corresponds to my experience of the writing journey: it is as if Pen(elope) and I secretly run off together to be joined in a kind of holy (or spiritual) matrimony – a union of mind and heart and the oneness I trust is our inherent nature and relationship with all of life.

When putting this book together, I further got curious about the name Penelope and learned that it has origins in Ancient Greek, means *weaver* and that Penelope was the wife of Odysseus, the legendary hero in Greek mythology.

According to Homer's account in his epic poem, The Odyssey, Penelope waited twenty years for her husband to return home from his journey. Despite over a hundred suitors wooing her, she remained true to Odysseus and, for this reason, the name has come to be associated with faithfulness. I was very glad to be reminded of this because it resonated deeply with how I viewed my relationship with my writing muse. In Homer's work, Penelope is further portrayed as an embodiment of patience, strength and cunning. These qualities are also ones Pen (elope) cultivates in me through the gift of writing.

Another interesting detail in connection with the meaning *weaver*, is the weaving ruse Penelope used to deter suitors: she pretended to be weaving a burial shroud for Odysseus's elderly father Laertes, announcing that she will choose a suitor when she has finished. Yet, each evening she would unravel her work and thus could cunningly delay re-marrying. Similarly, I experience the process of writing as a kind of weaving that never really ends. When writing, I get to interlace words and sometimes get to glimpse (if only briefly) at the inter-connected, cohesive whole that is the fabric of life. As soon as that moment is over, it is as if all has been unraveled and I begin again in front of a fresh loom and a new piece of writing. How many times have I inwardly celebrated what I consider a personal breakthrough, to wake up the next day (or next moment) to an empty loom and no other choice than to begin again - setting off once more, as if for the first time, my only guides: trust in the process and the faithfulness of Pen (elope).

Every piece included in the book has its unique place. Together, as a collection, the work is witness to the various flows and currents, turning of tides and points of orientation that can lead me to a larger, more connected and wholesome way of being in the world. I have purposely put the pieces in a loose order that is neither chronological, nor necessarily showing progression to a particular place (state) or conclusion; I have experienced the writing journey as far from orderly or cohesive. I would describe the process more like diving, sinking, floating, or spinning around and around and the overall progress, a spiraling - passing the same (or similar) place over and over, each time being given a chance to discover different meanings, views and perspectives not noticed before.

The intentions for creating this book are:

❖ as reminder of the spiritual quests I have been on to discover my true, authentic self;

❖ as a way of honouring the writer in me, in others and the sacredness of life itself;

❖ as a reminder of the above when I forget or get lost along the way.

I am thrilled every time any of my writing can inspire others, or provide nourishment to heart and soul. In that spirit, I hope you will find this book uplifting and encouraging.

POEMS ALL THE WAY

Hands

I thank you, hands
for holding this pen,
for turning this page,
for opening this door
and - for being here -
without conditions.

I thank you, hands
for reminding me of
tickling, caressing,
praying and dancing,
and for a simple touch:
hands on heart.

I thank you, hands.
I have been blessed by you
and with you
I can bless, too.

Muses of a Creative

It is my business to create – a business fated to those of sensitive hearts and perceiving eyes. I question all things I see – not with intellectual mind or scientific approach, not with skill or knowledge of current affairs, history, or economy - There is a knowing that is invisible. It comes in through my eyes, invisible; slips down my throat, invisible and does work in the dark, invisible. My business is to create: make visible the invisible, make tangible the intangible and make comprehensible the incomprehensible. At least it is my business to try. Try I must, for that is my call: call to create.

I have woken up

to the sight of snowflakes floating past my kitchen window; specks of softness on the other side of the pane. Yet in my messy mind, I am lost amid to-do lists, unfinished jobs, stalled projects and plans for the future. They waddle and hop, squabble and peck at me like vicious geese. And I am sent out into the blizzard of all that I am not, all that I never will be and all ways I am insufficient and shameful. So very shameful. Outside, all the while, snowflakes glide down to the ground, become a bright white lawn. I open my arms as if to catch some and instead catch my breath. And in that brief pause, I hear snowflake's song:

It's
simple, they sing,
breath is here to breathe you,
we are here to teach you
how to go easy,
how to settle down,
how to come home to
yourself.

Lion on the Sofa

You loaf there limp and lonely,
paws: jumbo fur balls off woolen limbs,
mane: a frowsy poodle's coat.

You sneaked through
my house after dark
and plonked down – a dream gift
to unwrap in the morning.

With ruffled, cuddly-toy look, you lure
my fingers to your dreadlocked coat.
Does your drooping jaw contain
real lion teeth?
Your fluffy paws,
real lion claws?

Your fierce glance is lost
in the frenzy of my fingering.
My mind is lost in compassion
- as it often is –
for all living things
in dreams and
in the waking world.

Who are you?
Certainly not Aslan the Great Lion?
The Cowardly Lion from Oz, perhaps?
Or does your foot hold a thorn
I have overlooked?

It becomes a game.
I dance around you,
excited with my new toy,
eager to unravel great mysteries
from the dreamworld.

I had forgotten:
you are lying on my sofa;
you are my dream,
my lion.

Where is the wildness?
That grand roar?
Power and majesty?

I cannot remember.
I am far from home.
I am not just lying on the sofa,
I lie in the real world -

I care for all living things
except one.

A Cup of Yogi Tea

On my tea-bag label this morning, the message:
Do not feed the fears!
I have to laugh. It is still early and
I have faithfully fed a family of ten:

Fear of failing to live my life well
Fear of letting others down
Fear of procrastination
Fear of neglecting my body
Fear of growing old and frail and ill
Fear of confusion, and mindless living
Fear of losing all I love or hold dear
Fear of not responding to the call to write
Fear of living from my limited human mind
Fear of not truly living from the heart
Fear of not touching the divine.

Then comes the refreshing cup of tea

and a second reading of my thoughts.

This time, I recognise the f-signs
and know
I need not
follow them.

Sun Salutations

Surya[3] still rests
as I clear some space
(and my voice) at the crest
of the hill; I remove my shoes,
sharp sticks and stones
from the ground
and stand
tadasana[4] tall,
hands
palm to palm:

Om Suryaya Namaha[5]

Arms reaching up, I greet Sky.
Body bending down, I greet Earth.
Legs lunging back, I greet Water.
Hips up, then down, I greet Mountain,
I greet Lake.
Flat on the grass,
I greet Worm,
I greet Snake.
Standing tall once more,
I greet Tree, Forest, Bird, Bee
and include myself:

---

[3] *Surya*, sanskrit meaning sun.
[4] *Tadasana*, sanskrit meaning 'mountain pose' or 'tree pose'
[5] *Om Suryaya Namaha* - a mantra to the sun which honours the sun as life giver, a masculine force that dispels darkness and brings activity and transformation through light, heat and fire.

I greet Me,
I greet You
I greet All
who do not believe
we belong
or have forgotten
we live with this
one same sun, this
one same breath.

No matter what we tell ourselves,
we are here,
in deep - all of us -
invitees.

Your Birthday

All that was important was to sit with you.
No timetable. No 'things' to do - Just sit. Spend time.
Sixteen hours of space.

You didn't understand much I said, or remember
I now lived in Italy. You didn't know I would leave later,
or that it was our last day together.

You kept forgetting your age, that you were unable to
walk, shave, dress, or visit the bathroom
without the help of nurses.

You just knew moments, snap-shots of
past, present and you found the
sense of it all
in the patterns of your dressing gown.

Julie Andrews beaches
in Wales   the
Tenors   your
daught-   ter's
voice old family house

You followed the checkered lines with your index finger
and stored them there:
forever!
I may have been with you for just an hour,
for a week, a year, or had never left home at all.

To you, it was all the same
time.

In this place, you have everything you need: peace.

Thank you, Daddy for your 87th birthday gift to me.

Softy

You sweet, smooth softy,
snug inside your shell -
outside,
the fast, furious world
turns in crisis,
screams for help,
begs attention.
Your telescope eyes
barely find extension.

You sweet, smooth softy
silent inside your shell -
outside,
the crazy, complex world
turns in circles,
sobs for solace,
wants for action.
Your sense and sensitivity
barely find expression.

At least as long as
one million years, it seems
I have been spiralling
inside
these smooth, forgotten routes
steadily and alone.

The solution is simple:
feed me some salt
and I will die for you.

A Tea Party

I shall have a tea party and invite them. No point not inviting them. They'd barge in anyway, Maleficent-style. So, I will invite them and I'll be polite and offer them some tea with plenty of sugar. Yes, I'll ask them in and sit them down and let them vent their complaints. I will listen. I will listen the way children listen to a nagging parent. I'll let the wind of their words pass softly through and take some of the cobwebs away. Yes, I really do think this is the best plan: a spring-cleaning tea party; just me and the two of them. No need to invite the others. I shall seat Seamus Shame on my right and Gilbert Guilt on my left and I will smile pleasantly. I will offer them home-baked buns topped with icing and a cherry. I will pretend to like their company and I will be very friendly. All the time I will be spring-cleaning and their voices will drone on in the background like a train drones across a wide valley. Yes, I shall invite them to my exclusive, afternoon, spring-cleaning tea party and we'll sip tea together and eat buns. There will be music in my head as their rhythmic chatter diddledy-dees and diddledy-dums through the valley of my mind - a passing train - an express: a noisy but short disturbance. Then, I will open my eyes and my house will be quiet and clean and I will look out into my garden and see the exquisite brightness of spring's greens and yellows and pinks.

Alchemy?

Bear, tell me:
are these Merlin's tricks you play?
Or have you made mercury
from this diamond
and that furry
hump of yours?

I float, buoyant, light
on silvery beads
whilst your bulk
lurks
ambivalent
in the shadows.

Where is your power?
That roar?
Are you resting,
or are you prowling
and ready to pounce
at the first sign
of my ignorance
and the next step
on this journey
to gold?

March

The old lady's door is open.
A sign of spring?
It says: I invite you in,
we'll drink *espresso* and chat a while.

I hide in my kitchen
unready to leave my winter den.
I am still dressed in grey,
ugly duckling that I am.

Despite primroses on the sills
and twenties in the sun,
Swan has not yet come.
I continue to hibernate.
Lonely *nonna*[6] will have to wait.

---

[6] nonna is Italian for grand-mother.

Breaking the Fast

This morning I lay down
in your cereal bowl
under morsels of kiwi,
under the Country Crisp.

Crunching through
will you taste
the softness
after your tongue has licked
sour fruit,
frostbitten to sweetness,
underneath it all?

Harvesting

This year, the best year ever
for beans. The green and strong
fagiolini[7], the long and wide
piattoni[8]; some skinny, some fat,
all ripe and bulging
like meat morsels
on the pizza I prepare,
filled with good will
and goodness: protein, riboflavin et al.
Vitamins A, C, K,
folate and phosphorus,
magnesium and manganese.

My own harvest: this heart beat -
I connect to self-compassion and
deep living in moments like these:
picking beans, washing and slicing,
steaming and frying -
freezing in bags for winter.

I harvest self-knowledge, too
through food for thought,
for growth and next spring,
hoping to blossom
and bear fruit
other colours than green.

---

[7] Fagiolini, the Italian term for string beans or French beans.
[8] Piattoni, a type of Italian runner bean or flat bean.

Me and My Beanstalk

Bean *prana*[9],
full of energy,
of vital force:
potential to expand,
reach for the sky
like bean stalks do as they climb
and like Jack's did
and mine does too
now that my cow has been sold and
I can stretch up high and
dig down deep
into fertile ground

and feel
how Earth and Heaven
are real,
how they heal,
how they lift me
to other gardens,
other harvests,
other realms
beyond imagining,
beyond what mind calls -
'The best you will ever get!'

---

[9] Prana is Sanskrit meaning breath or life force that permeates all levels of reality.

Queen of Middle Age

I don't go on diets
I don't believe they work

but when I grew
the dreaded
middle-aged spread,
I decided I must
reconsider my view,
try something new,
new being:

The 50+ Diet:

- Ballet and buns for breakfast
- A lion of a lunch (yogic style)
- Skip through dinner
- At night: dine on dreams.

Now that I have shed
all the extra weight,
I like to be seen
and feel
like a Queen
of Middle Age
with added guarantee:
I start each day
with a round *beat*
rooted in my heart.

Soft Fruit Season

The soft fruits have arrived
from the south. Market stalls
have transformed customers' gazes
and baste in the brightness
of the red beauties:
Raspberry,
Redcurrant,
Strawberry...

How bold you are!
You demand attention,
attract many a mouth and purse
to open wide, hands
to dip in, tongues
to wrap around
your juiciness.

Senses dance easily
in soft fruit season.

How I wish to be dancing
in tune to this harvest;
yet I find myself in a season
of a different kind -

Rosacea has arrived
and is announcing it to the world
through inflamed cheeks
that burn, scream for attention
and win
the red competition.

My soft animal inside
has scurried away and
curled into a ball
like a young hedgehog
whose outer spines are in place,
but not yet strong to
make an adequate defense;
not yet matured to
embody the wisdom:
'There is nothing to be defended!'

What is Your Teaching, Body?

I have read that the body
is a learning lab,
that this flesh
is not who I am

but mind wants
to possess it and calls it me

and I see skin in anguish, in distress;
eyes looking out of puffy lids,
red like my rash and
full of folds,
as if zoomed into old age
in just a few days.

I wish to age
with grace and compassion
but what about this:
blemishes, spots, wrinkles;
mind looking on, judging,
calling me 'ugly', 'shameful'?

How to speak kindly
when feeling thin-walled and crumpled;
when feeling pummeled and knuckled;
when feeling split, ripped off centre,
capillaries spidering my face?
I know these veins, like stains
will not remove easily.

How do I still love her,
still hold her close,
still care enough to allow her
to be here?

What is your teaching, body?

Breathe with her!
Rub ointment into your sore skin;
caress with a tender voice
and speak deep into her ear
so that she hears without a doubt:
'You are unique and complete.
I love you just as you are.'

In the midst of this anguish,
let the sunlight in
and fertilise your own soil,
feed seeds of trust

for all that is fragile inside,
for all that needs to be seen.

All of us are in season and
can be harvested
as we are,
lifting us beyond (yet not making us immune to)
scorn and scrutiny
for being as we are
for being
ultimate vulnerability.

What Body Has to Say

I am here for healing.
I am here for you whilst you are here.
Listen!
Listen well!
Listen again!

that rumbling,
that grumbling,
that aching,
that paining,
that straining,
that bleeding,

that problem of the body...

...that is not who you are!

that discomfort,
that disturbance,
that disgust,
that distress,
that discord,
that disease,

that long list of all that is wrong...

...that is not who you are!

we are messengers
passing through,
rapping on your head,
knocking on your knees,

rattling your bones,
boiling your blood,
twisting your back,
pulling your arm,
scratching your skin,

trying to get in
to where you hide,
deep inside,

where you shine
beyond the limiting mind,
beyond the limited body,
beyond all limits
beyond space and time.

Shadow and I

I shall not entertain
jumping over my shadow;
I shall jump in
like a child jumps into a puddle -
in and out,
in and out.

I shall entertain
wallowing in puddles.
I will wallow away
like a pig in mud -
over and over,
over and over.

I entertain
jumping into puddles.
We jump together
like dolphins in oceans -
in and out,
up and over.

I stop entertaining
and we leap -
we leap
unlike any way we have leapt before -
high and beyond.

Wholly Human

It's strange to be human!
I look, observe, wishing to see
who I am, who we are;
odd creatures we are.
I do not know or understand
who I am, who you are;
yet I do catch glimpses -
in moments like this,
whilst writing, feeling alive,
connected to life.

It's human to be human!
I become quiet and ask:
Who am I?
Who are we?
I do not know or understand
and catch myself thinking
I am not at home,
or welcome in this world.

Is there an explanation for this?

I do a little research
and discover: only human
beings feel this way;
honey bees don't.

So, why can't I be
'just me'-
a plain human being
without the trimmings?

An answer does not come,
but imagination does,
in the form of mercury.
I am suddenly entering
a tub filled to the brim.

There are no sides,
no bottoms, no tops -
just a mass of silvery blobs
that flow and merge
this way and that.

Another moment of imagination
and I know I can let go -
I will not fall down.

Perhaps I will fall out
and into the whole
like a droplet from an ocean wave
sprayed skyward,
then landing
back in the water
from which it was
never separate.

View from a Heart

I am called to return
like an artist is called
to an unresolved painting;
one that has been brushed over and over
by a dissipated heart,
wiped out
then held,
suspended and ambivalent
- waiting -
for just the right light,
for just the right perspective,
for an unveiling.

I visit the boat –
the one moored by the trees,
leaning in close to see inside,
hair dipping into her portholes
down to the hull
where lifejackets and
ropes are stowed.

And my brush loads
with all the greys and browns and blues
of taupe,
of shadow and chagrin -
A world of lost depth and contrast
moving as it must
through such weather conditions
like my heart,
at times,
hanging out there
on those feint lines

between ocean and sky,
between boat and shore
among watercolour clouds:
the only lighthouse
guiding me home.

On Being Human

Being human
is perfectly fine
as it is
and in the larger picture of things,
everything that happens
is perfectly fine
as it is

human experience:
choiceless
awareness, an all-inclusive
package. There are options
but no option boxes
to cross and stop
those feelings,
and all
we wish
would not
come up
as it does -

and it does
as it does
and you have to take it
or leave it –
no amendments
or embellishments -
it simply is what it is
and does as it does
and here is
the hitch:

shame arises and
there is nothing you can do
- it just is
and wants to be
embraced
by our being,
like it is,
like it or not
you can have an opinion
but, you really have
no choice but to accept it
as it is.

So, when shame comes,
the most important thing
to remember is this:
not to judge yourself
for the shame,
for the woes,
for the emotion
contained in it all
but to simply sit
and let it be
perfectly fine
as it is
until you can feel
it is as it is
to the very core
of your human
beingness.

Love in the Lawn

We stand outside, toes touching
the innersoles of muddy shoes,
bodies bathed in out-of-doors sound:
kreee, cheee, breees, streeem...

A symphony of insects and imaginings:
seeds opening, sap shooting skyward
like fizzy pop, fireworks and Prosecco corks -
all under the surface of our lawn.

Our shears cut through stems
that once held beeblossoms,
hands light like Aero and Maltesers;

Ah, fast blood, speeding legs -
How youth was full
of spaciousness, I remember:

I had set out to write a poem
about relationship,
about the way it has swung
up and down over the years
like the children's swing and slide;
how our marriage,
like the wooden sun loungers,
has turned silver.

I receive what comes,
whispered by the ground
under my feet:

Barefooted, love is real in the garden,
and side by side - brushing shoulders,
paths and teeth together - shopping,
putting out the rubbish
on Mondays.

I take off my shoes,
walk on the grass
and take off my glasses,
rubbing them over and over
with a Kleenex,
taking away the smears and
any doubt around the question:
were we meant for each other?

Under the Waxing Moon

Under the waxing moon
we stand, smoke curling
skyward into the night,
rising from cigarettes
I do not smoke;
yet here I am,
smoking -
under Great Bear - Ursa Major -
wondering
what it all means.

It's cold,
I wear a blanket
and drink grappa with you -
Nonnino - small grandpa -
freezing, yawning, awing.

The fire awaits inside -
cosy by the flames,
our fingers play.

There's a light, a glow,
filled with frivolity.

It's been decades:
two thirds of a lifetime -
hands, bodies -
all fiery together.

Dream Spirit

I am Shaman. Old Man of the Sea,
come on a journey in the dream world with me!
We'll sail to the source, to secrets untold
and on to new waters - Come now, be bold!

I am Medicine Man, I know how to heal,
I'll show you what's false and also what's real;
I'll soul-doctor your hurts with medicinal brews,
bring hope and humility to all aspects of you.

I am Fairytale Story, yet also Nightmare,
battle you will, fear and pain you will bear;
sometimes as hero, just as much as a fool.
I dare you, enter the adventure dream-pool!

I am Fisherman of the Deep, Turner of Great Tides;
I'll take you fathoms down, or on waves, let you ride.
I'll twirl you and spin you and present at your feet,
all of your inner sea-monsters and beasts.

I am Mystery, I am Magic and Eternity;
I know about your strengths and your fragility;
and I know that the future downfall of man
will be when he's forgotten
the Great Old Shaman.

Life in Prints

I have filled many notebooks over the years bought in the UK, Germany, France, Luxembourg, Switzerland, Spain, Italy, the US, Canada, India... perhaps even more countries than these. They contain my words - tracks and marks I have made as I have journeyed to places, seen and done various things on my path through life. In them, I have philosophised, criticised, fantasised and analysed, all the while hoping to understand who I am. What I have said in these books is possibly less important than the process I have been through whilst making the marks. I call it 'making footprints'. One day I will look back and I will know that, regardless of whether there is a single one of my prints to be seen, the journey will have been worth it, because I will have learned to love my smelly, blistered human feet and my very vulnerable and sensitive human heart.

Yes and No Game

Yes:

misty, magical
moonlit man
metaphor and myth-musings
magnificent mountains
meaningfulness
marvellous mystery

No:

miserly, mechanical
mindset man
monstrous matters
mournful moments
meaninglessness
miserable mastery.

Mare Nostrum

Poor Mediterranean, full of man's rubbish! I see
another carrier bag (Oh, how my green heart hurts!) –
it bobs there, translucent below the surface; handles
like strips of lure: death food to innocent fish.
Such disrespect!
I contemplate all the pollution of our Earth
and the unheeded pleas for it to stop.

Men's cries pierce my meditation:
sharp like arrows, they fly fast and far
from their luxury yacht.
Sun glares in my eyes.
I tread water and shoot back:
"The ocean's not a dump! You hear? Not a dump!"
The men flail and scream their French:
"Non madame! Non madame! Attention! Attention!
Meduse! Meduse!"

My heart bangs a fierce rhythm,
drums me into trance. Siren-like,
yet in utter silence, she serenades
- filigree strings reeling me in
to her blue, pulsing heart.
I am prey and lover:
we dance a perilous pas-de deux
and I see deep into her eyes -

A simple vision: we are One.

Rich Mediterranean, full of deep knowing!

Onset of Spring

Do not endeavour to grow
a new pair of wings;
those you have are fine.
Just cradle the one in the other a while
and sing a lullaby:
a Rock-a-bye Baby or two,
till both cheer and smile
themselves to full plume.

Do not endeavour to fly
up and away with your wings;
where you are now is fine.
Just let them open
an inch at a time
to feel wind's breath
- the gentle tug
like strings to a kite,
till both lift to the skies
with eagle, swan and delight.

Where are you going so hastily?

"Where are you going so hastily?"
says the path to her feet.

"We want to reach the top
of this steep hill, see the sun
as she sinks
and glimpse
the first evening star."

"Tell her that if she's after
that special one,
she's better
staying home - That star
will soon shine
from up there
through her window
where she stands,
hands deep
in the sink."

Poetry on the Lake

Willow, how you hang deep and low,
stretching or simply resting
in a forward bow?
Are you drowsing? Sleeping?
Or are you really weeping?
Your branches are hanging,
tips are dipping;
dipping and sipping, sipping and dipping,
then dancing and swaying
like arms of ballerinas,
necks, long and strong
like the swan:

Mute Swan, quietest of all,
rarely a chatter or a call.
You glide, you ride
the waterways and lakes,
gently make partings;
a rippling and a whirling,
floating, without fussing –
riding and flowing,
like you're blessing just by being;
simply your presence - quiet quiescence –
dripping and seeping,
often times pouring
into the water.

Wings tucked in or held high
on your back, then that crack
and that whip, huge spans
start to flap
and you dash down the lake,
plumage fluttering, bright bill tilting, lifting
upwards, black knob throbbing, feet slapping
and turning,
your whole body working,
speeding, then reaching
the moment of flying,
wings still moving,
still audibly calling;
wailing and waving,
celebrating this takeoff -

your weight now soaring.

Willow gently bowing,
understanding this language,
and nature all around her.

I just sit
watching,
witnessing,
listening,
grateful, so grateful
to be able to be here -

No more needed.

Imagine This!

Imagine this!
All you have gathered,
stored and stashed;
all you have thought
was you, only you;
all your squirrelled things:
attainments, perceptions,
memories, stories, on and on...

Everything gone!
Finished!

Who are you then?

Imagine
meeting yourself
right there
in the middle
of that thought!

No 'thing' added -
No 'thing' subtracted.

Imagine! Nothing
between you and You–

Imagine!
Imagine!
Imagine!

Dear Gardener,

For years, you have been harvesting me, taking me into your hands and peeling back my layers: my shabby and worn-out skins; the too thick ones, the too thin ones. You relentlessly strip off the bad, the bitter, the poisonous and false and take pride in revealing all my imperfections and blemishes. You say these are the best bits – the goodness – and what you will always find at the core of me, at the core of all of us. In your hands, I grow full of human beingness and flourish in this garden: Life.

It's Official

Today is the day
you have been,
once again reborn
into eternal youth.
Oh spring!
How you startle us,
your secret substance
suddenly on display,
shimmering,
scintillating,
so full of surprises,
and you, Mimosa,
surprised by March snow,
as were other trees,
did not snap in two,
did not break your bow;
you simply bent down
and let those fluffy fingers,
sweep the snow
from your feet
whilst you continued to sing
your scent of spring
into the air
and the heavy load
slowly slipped off.

Now you stand up straight,
blushing
a bright lemon yellow
for us all.

Eavesdropping

Eavesdropping on my mind
like I am eavesdropping
on this tree, ears up
to the canopy,
listening to the leaves.

I hear the fluttering, the flapping,
flurries of hurried discussions
on and off, loud, then soft:
all-around sound.

Eavesdropping on Earth,
ear close to the ground,
I hear:
Worm speak worm,
Grass speak grass,
Root speak root,

and I know
how mind is
free like the wind;
it can make noise
and heave whole trees
out of the ground;
it can gently breeze,
creating peace and ease
all around, as easily as
the wind can dance
with the leaves.

Venus and Moon Mind the Night

These past nights
Venus shines wide
beside a waning moon,
her light-year rays
reach into my bedroom,
pick the lock
on my mind
and illuminate
all the nonsense inside –

like, we reside
on solid ground,
separate and
far apart.

How absurd it seems, these nights,
that I have ever believed
a single word
my mind has ever said.

By Water's Edge

It is silence,
silence I yearn -
and I wonder
how is death?
Is it peaceful,
peaceful and
light?

It is ease,
ease I yearn -
and I sink
to the depths.
Yes!
It is peaceful
here.

It is lightness,
lightness I yearn -
and I bubble
up from the bottom,
back up
to the light.

It is air,
air I yearn -
and I breathe:
in and out,
in and out.

It is joy,
joy I yearn -
and I smile

I smile
I smile

silence.

Moon Meditation

Gather your attention,
gather your scattered seeds;
pick them up
with care
and care
for all
that has brought you here:
all that has grown
you into you.

Stand under the light
of any moon;
full, or less full,
visible or not.

See those seeds flit
night after night
like fireflies,
dancing magically,
magnificently
and
alighting
here and there
on darkness,
or in your palms
as you reach out.

If Conditions

If I were spirit, I'd call myself Divine Love.
I would only live in the soul
and I would be invisible –
but I am not.

If I were voice, I'd call myself Song.
I would live anywhere
and I would be audible –
but I am not.

If I were source, I'd call myself Silence.
I would live everywhere
and I would be untouchable –
but I am not.

If I were surrender, I'd call myself Here.
I would live nowhere.
I would simply be here.
But?

No more buts: here I am!

End of story!

Dropping the Tissue

On this journey along the path of life
I met Gangaji[10] and sat
Satsang[11] with her and Eli.

She took a tissue out of a box,
made a fist and
pushed it inside.
A moment later,
She opened it once more,
and the trapped multi-ply,
uncurled and floated
to the floor.

"This is how to let go," she said.

How simple, how poetic!
I thought, and in an instant, saw:
just how much I had been holding on;
just how much I had been doing;
just how much I was trapped
inside my own mind
holding on tight
to that tissue
longing to simply let go.

---

[10] Gangaji is an American born spiritual teachers who regularly holds Satsang in different countries around the world with her husband Eli Jackson-Bear.
[11] Satsang is a Sanskrit term meaning "being in the company of the truth" or "right association," and refers to a group of like-minded people who engage in a spiritual dialogue.'

And I felt myself open,
ready and willing to fully
go through with it
once and for all;
I was just going to
'drop my tissue'.

And guess what?
Immediate success and
the end of my issues
with life and suffering?

No, no, no - absolutely not!

Just a mind trying very hard
to pry itself open and the tissue
tightening into a ball inside.

Days go by, months, years
and out of the blue, I notice:
absence of tension in the jaw,
absence of tension in the heart,
absence of tension in the hands;

I feel light and alive and free:
'tissues' galore
slip from my mind
and release poetically
to the floor.

Metamorphosis

Stay!
Wait!
All cold winter long.
She will come.
She <u>will</u> come.
And with her, the knowing
that you and she are
one
magnificent swan.

Today I Awake

Today I awake and all is jumbled
as if life had been placed
on my bedside table and the whole lot
tipped whilst I was sleeping.

All is in a heap.

I do not know when, how or if
I was ever born; where I have or
have not been; which words
I may or may not have uttered
up to now – yesterday even.

What about tomorrow?

Memory and knowledge,
past, present and future
spin inside my head:
a trillion particles, patterns and traces
from time's dusty old carpet.

All is meaningful, I am sure;

yet lost in a mind
that refuses to understand
wholeness
and the turning
of universes.

Coming Back

Back home in my house,
in my bed, in my life
after a week away –
after this brief absence,
coming back is hard –
like learning to dance
a new dance;
a dance that has changed.

I walk into my home –
'present and correct'
says the mirror
when it 'sees' me
standing here again
in the very same spot.

At my friend's place,
I had gathered my belongings,
said goodbye and left.
In front of her mirror,
I had felt 'present and correct', too.

Did I leave something on the train?
Did an important piece
of the complex puzzle I call me,
go missing, or get lost?

Yes, perhaps, it did, says the mirror:
though your presence is apparent,
it seems a part is often absent.

Under the Bodhi Tree[12]

I sit under the Bodhi tree
and bow to you, Namo[13].
I name you, Namo:
sad, sad, sad.

You sit under the Bodhi tree
And bow to me, Namo.
You name me, Namo:
sad, sad, sad.

We sit under the Bodhi tree
And bow and bow, Namo
We name ourselves, Namo:
sad, sad, sad.

I sit under the Bodhi tree
And bow to you, Namo
We are with you, Namo
You are with us, Namo:

glad, glad, glad.

---

[12] Bodhi Tree is the sacred fig tree in Bodh Gaya under which the Buddha, Siddhartha Gautama, is said to have attained enlightenment.

[13] Namo comes from Sanskrit (and Pali) and means "veneration" or "homage" or "adoration" or "with utmost respect, honour and admiration," It is used before announcing the names of Buddha and Bodhisattvas..

At my Open Door

I stand at my open door – unexpectedly.
The guest arrives like a caring friend,
opens her arms and pulls me to her - a snug fit.
I welcome her in.

Inside, in the dark, her arms close around me
and like a cunning enemy,
tighten and squeeze love out
as easily as puss from a zit.

She takes hold of my own hand and
slaps me with it: slap after slap, after slap.
Crimson with rage, my spirit beseeches:
Step out of the way! Let her pass through!

The guest leaves
as she came –
unexpectedly.

Feeling What we are Feeling

We can appear fragile, even to ourselves.
Sickness and disease are real
and mortality is a truth of life
that is healthy to remember daily.

You see what is imperfect in me
and still you love that part;
hold it, hold me, patiently,
confident I am finding my way;
no longer fantasising,
no longer needing to be different,
fixed, or moulded into
something else.

We need to be appreciated,
acknowledged and must know
we all belong;
that there is a unique place
for each and every one.
But we must meet life as whole beings,
fully allow ourselves to feel
what we are feeling.

Day after Day of Downpour

Day after day of downpour tore
our small world asunder:
ponds became lakes,
brooks became torrents,
roads became rivers;
waters ran wild, sending land sliding,
walkways slipping and
mud running down the hill
into our home.

I sit and ponder this flooding
while the sun shines and
the water recedes as if nothing
had happened; oak leaves warm themselves
before their autumn release
and their final glide down
to the ground they will become.

I realise that I must recede too
and I will not drown.

Red Admiral alights on dried bracken
close by and grants me courage.
There he rests,
no spring or summer camouflage;
nothing to hide his beauty.
In plain sight, on bare ferns,
in colours unmistakably his,
he dares to be seen and admired.

How to Joy Ride

So much has been going on
in this still place:
joy is arriving,
tip-toeing in.

A kind voice says*:*

Joy never left
like the breath that
never stops breathing you.

A smile doesn't come easily.
A mindless moment and here is Judge.

I have been told I can choose:
get in Judge's car,
or let it pass by:

All you need do
is retract the thumb.

So, for once, I follow
the instructions.

No thumb - No hitch

and get to joy ride!

Up with the Larks

I am singing, rejoicing, in exaltation -
up with the larks, lofty and light.
What a delight to be walking this morning
up to the chapel and view -
atop the hill of San Quirico[14].

High above village, home and lake,
spring in each step, wide, smiling strides -
heart leading, generous and full,
chest open -

Any treasure?

Hello Oak and Birch, Bramble and Bee!
Hello Dead Leaves from last autumn!
Have you been feeding the forest floor?

Yes, I know, it has not been easy;
conditions are sometimes harsh;
yet, I see the fruit:
bright green and sprightly prickled.

This year's chestnuts will be good!

---

[14] San Quirico is the name of a chapel and wooded hill surrounding it. The chapel is situated on a hilltop along the shore of Lago Maggiore in the province of Varese, Italy

Thoughts and I

How you exhaust me, self-critical thoughts!
How many years
have you been shouting,
loud and foul-mouthed,
carpet beaters in hand
beating the living star dust out of me?

Are you not sorry for all the pain
you have caused?

Ma'am, we have served you all our lives,
faithful and forever on call. Day and night
we have done our work – for you -
We have kept you separate and small
as you commanded us to do.

You are not the one enslaved.
It is us who are captives in your mind
and long for our release.
You may dismiss us whenever you like
and we'll forever leave you in peace.

Oh no, not that way!
It has to be soft and from the heart.
No yelling, or ordering us to go away.
That will be our cue to stay.

Say, 'Thank you, my dear friends,
I appreciate all you have done.
And to show how much I care,
I release you now with kindness,

not regret, or with a grudge to bear.

It may at first feel strange inside –
a stillness as if dear ones have died.
But please don't call us back
because we will come if you call
and be there in a flash,
carpet beaters and all.

Ushered In?

Mouths water for a reason
so do eyes (as hearts bleed).

Imagine
all this fluid
seeping into Earth,
sloshing this way,
sloshing that way.

Is this the law
that forces
gates to open?
Like arms of a sluice
open,
waters gush in
without us knowing
what is happening;
how we are being
ushered in
to be here
together?

Shopping for Cheese

Shopper in hand, I walk towards the shop with a mission:
to buy the cheese (low in lactose) sold here and here only.

I stride past an unkempt man with a mongrel at his feet
and a sign I cannot miss or misunderstand:

Wir haben Hunger!

I catch the words, askance, walking as I am,
brisk-paced, unwilling to delay or deviate from my fixed plan.

The doors slide apart, lure me in off the streets;
yet I hover there, hesitant...
and turn back.

"Worauf haben Sie Hunger?"

He opens his mouth, closes his mouth, looks right, looks left
like someone hesitant to cross a main road...
and responds:

"Ich habe einen Kochtopf!"

Strange reply!

"Möchten Sie Wurst?"

"Nein, ich mag keine Wurst."

Fussy man! Why had I bothered to ask?

"Brot? Käse?"

He settles for:
Gruyère cheese in a block, not sliced.
Wrapped in paper, not cling film.
Rye bread, the sour-dough kind, no yeast.
Sliced but no plastic bag.

I move through the aisles with my judging mind,
and a new mission: to see the human side; to see him -
someone just like me:
a vegetarian with intolerances,
a cheese lover,
someone who cares about the environment.

I buy not one, but two packs of Gruyère
and choose the best-quality sourdough rye they have.

 "Gruyère! Gruyère! Danke! Danke!

He shakes my hand, surprising me now with English:

"You remind me of a woman. I help her. She arrive in
Germany. She cannot speak German. I speak English. I help
her. Today you help me. You look just like her. I help once, I
did. I help. Once."

I shake his hand and leave –
without the cheese I came for,
but with my face saying cheese
and that loaf of a mind in tow.

An Age, 26

26, an age
to give life...

The age you gave life to me.
The age I gave life
to a son and you, a daughter -
for you, the third of four;
for me, the first of two.

We were joined in that moment
whether we knew it or not
through the umbilicus -
a chord as soft as a whisper, as a song;
as a line of verse across ages,
across generations.

26, an age
to give life...

We reached out to touch
one another - mother to mother -
child to child - child to mother
and all mothers
down a line and back
to the very first one
to carry a child
in a womb.

26, an age
to give life…

The first simple
gift of life
from one to another;
the giving of bodies,
the giving of souls,
the giving of love:
the joy of a mother.

26, an age
to give life…

Over and over
this need
to reach,
to teach,
to tell
our stories
- all of them -

across lines,
across time,
through mothers
and love
and in the name
of human kind.

Everywhere and Nowhere

Are we not all (secretly)
going somewhere?
Hoping we are somebody?
Going everywhere but nowhere?

Moved to write this, who am I?
Where am I going?

I am moving in close,
close to the ground.

I am listening out
for the patter of ants.

I am stepping aside,
letting them go on

as I go on, heart in my feet
with each throb of a poem

in my being.

I am feeling
cells buzzing,
their fullness,
their essence.

I am hearing
words speaking
their secret teachings

telling me I am being;
I am being who I am.

I am going somewhere
and that is nowhere:

Now-Here.

I am a Weeping Woman

I am a weeping woman. I weep on the inside.
I weep on the outside. I weep for me. I weep for you.
I weep because I love.
I weep because I don't.
I make love and weep.

I weep for abuse, for disgust, for violence.
I weep for injustice, for shaming, for blaming
and all that is a violation.
I weep for segregation and exclusion.

I weep because it hurts.
I weep because it doesn't.
I weep for the powerless and the powerful,
the helpless and the helpful,
the useless and the useful.

I weep for miracles, for poems and for no words.
I weep for mother earth.
I weep for the oceans, for the mountains, for trees.

I weep for all that is being done
and all that is not being done.
I weep for tigers, for bees,
for bears and for every breath,
every drop of blood of every human soldier,
every warrior.

I weep for beaten horses and dogs,
for peoples, for children, for women, for men,
and for every boy and girl,

for every 'them' and 'they'
and all who cannot be themselves.

I am a weeping woman.
I am the woe in women.
I weep for those who cannot weep.
I weep for those who can.
I weep for those who are told they must, but cannot
and for those who can, but are told they must not.

I weep for every reason called 'no reason'.
I weep for the unspoken, unexpressed, invisible;
I weep for the spoken, expressed, visible.

I weep for the silence in the world and
the silenced woman in me, the silenced one
in every woman, in every man, in every
sentient being -
for this is what I do.

I do not think it up.
I weep to be true
to who I am.

I am
a weeping woman.

Beyond Measure

This presence
is a present,
a precious gift;
the eye within
the eye of
each breath,
not to forget
death:
as yet not here;
yet here you are
absolutely filled
with
life
beyond
measure.

Sister Love

Venus
looks out
from outer space
for the
Goldilocks Planet
we call Earth.

How very small
it seems,

she ponders,
yet also sees
how it is
'just right'
for all the life
it supports;

how it is
expanding,
making room
for more and more

awe.

Mama Universe
really did
create the ideal place
for all being:

a perfect home
for mankind to grow
beyond themselves
and into greater
sapiens sapiens.

As you Are

As you are;
come as you are
to this moment, now
and now again,
as you have never
before been that
you are now.

As you are;
meet yourself as you are
for the first time, now
and the last time,
as you have never
before been that
as you are now.

Say goodbye to yourself
as you are now;
and realise,
you are not
anything that is
not exactly
as you are now.

A Taste for Mu

Now I have a taste for Mu[15]
I am discovering:
Mu is everywhere!
And I know I can have
a taste of Mu
each and every new Mu day.

I can spoon Mu into my soup,
spread Mu onto my bread,
use Mu soap and Mu shampoo,
Mu toothpaste and perfume.
Guess what hangs in the loo?
Mu loo rolls, for sure!

I can wear my new Mu shoes
and wander through my new Mu life,
through Mu meadows
full of Mu cows and
I can bow and greet
all that is Mu
and
all that is Mu
can greet back:
Moo, it says:
Moo, Moo, Moo.

---

[15] Mu is the shorthand name of the first koan in a collection called the *Gateless Gate* or *Gateless Barrier* (Chinese, *Wumengua*; Japanese, *Mumonkan*), compiled in China by Wumen Huikai (1183-1260).

Haiku or 17-Syllable Floats?

New deck chairs are set
upright and empty, I
sit down for support.

There is a whirlpool
a stone's throw away, I see
my mind turning.

Her body is lithe
and she dances through the night:
quickstep towards life.

Bag with open zip
invites a thief to enter:
I hold hands to heart.

It's still dark at five -
I write through sunrise and dawn
and wake aliveness.

In this email is
a word in BLOCK capitals:
emotion travels.

Beech nuts have fallen
on my usual bike path -
I whine, but crunch through.

A tree warbler calls
below the weeping willow -
I am six and silent.

The sun burns bare legs
stretched out on long loungers:
a mosquito sings.

The wind was howling,
hitting the walls of her house:
talk to your echo!

Crows caw-caw outside
as flocks gather on telephone wires:
Pen won't speak to me.

A Japanese soup:
hot vermicelli noodles.
I taste inner peace.

A single ashtray
on an old, folding table.
Everything must pass.

Fresh roses wrapped up
in tin foil and polythene.
Love will persist now.

My fountain pen falls.
Black ink spills over the floor.
Life and death happen.

Ice-cream in autumn
feels too cool for outside -
inside is winter.

Ink stains my fingers –
numerous lines on my hands;
veins look blue outside.

A scoop, a taste; your
flavour is not who you are
but you become that.

Become intimate
with the clouds; stay present with
blinding light of suns.

POEMS ON SUNDAYS

A Poem on Sunday I

In this moment,
life is full of wonder.
Mind is outside
in the hammock,
resting.
Inside, Heart is
rocking to the beat
of Earth's pulse.

In this brief pause,
Trust and Faith
take Willingness
by the hand
and bring her back
to hold mine –

They say they know the way.

A Poem on Sunday II

I walk barefoot
in layer upon layer
of cloth: designs
from a conditioned
mind

and as I walk,
the long arms of
Judgment,
Disapproval,
Jealousy and
Distrust
lurch and grab and
pull
I feel all

u
  n
 r
   a
    v
    e
   l
 l
 i
 n
 g

Finally,
here
I
am:
stripped,
barely
standing
      in
          all
             this
b   r   i   g   h   t   n   e   s   s.

A Poem on Sunday III

Today I dress
in gratitude,
express
wordless
reverence
to this day.

This gossamer cloak
strokes
my restless
mind
and glides me
into being.

A Poem on Sunday IV

I have asked
that thy will be done,

that I may befriend
all I feel,
embrace my awkward,
confused self,
commit
to the words
You speak
and bow.

You whisper
here at lake's edge,
touching my fist
like bubbles -

I do not need
to will it open.
It simply opens
and I receive.

Beside Myself

I sit beside myself and pray
I will not become obsessed
and my hand holds the hand
of the part of me that sits apart.

I sit beside myself and whisper
"You are fine just as you are."
And we hold hands, side by side
till we find our way back home.

Some Sundays

Some Sundays, early
outside my bedroom,
trees are swaying,
planes are flying, booming
sounding lines into being.

I wonder, am I dreaming?
Am I waking and noticing
how much I am sleeping?

Morning has Broken

Kettle hums as it boils water and I hear the first cuckoo call.
A woodpecker joins, drumming on the old chestnut and
I remember how I loved the hymn we sang at assembly:

> *Morning has broken, like the first morning,*
> *Blackbird has spoken, like the first bird.*

I pour hot water on peppermint picked from the garden,
watch leaves swirl green into the cup.
Things stir in me, my cells start singing:

> *Aliveness has awoken, like the first dawning*
> *Cuckoo has spoken, like the first word.*

I am not religious. I was christened yet do not go to church.
Inside, I sense I am in there, I can even smell incense burning
and feel the vastness, the airy high space of the nave.

> *This is a good place to sit awhile, listen to poetry,*
> *receive blessings; drink holy water.*

Purple

Purple is the eve,
the wind's mood,
a sky soaking in sunset's bath:
it is a translucent pool
spilled wide across the dusk.

Purple is the night,
the mountain's shadow,
a wave rising to heaven's realm:
it is a mighty horse
released and free in the dark.

Purple is the dream,
a star's promise,
Earth glistening in silvery sleep:
it is an angel's embrace
fluffed in effervescent light.

Purple is the colour,
an artist's palette,
food for a fierce hunger:
it is plump inspiration
primed and ripe for the day.

Purple is the dawn,
sunrise's song;
a call to a writer's heart –
it is this moment of awe
and this bow,
to all of creation.

I Bow to the Peach Tree

I bow to the peach tree and gather
one of her fallen fruits.

I kneel among the beans
and pluck their offerings.
I imagine they are singing:

This is the last harvest of the season.

This evening I feel
how the moon must feel
when she wanes and
disappears into blackness.

Before I go to sleep,
I try not to forget that
I will also feel the delight
when she returns
full-to-bursting with light
and shines right back
into this dark room.

When you Come...When You Go

When you come,
please be brief;
take me off my guard, please do;
don't wait till I am wearing nappies,
have incoherent thought
and am unable to hold a spoon.

When you come,
please don't linger;
just let me go quietly, please do;
in a moment of clarity,
when I still know my family
and am able to say farewell, adieu.

When you go,
please be gentle;
leave in love and peace, please do;
tell them that all is right this way,
that I live on in their hearts
and the brightness of every
new moon.

Winter Meditation

May you be gentle and kind to
yourself.

May you embrace the timid and vulnerable inside.

May you remember that what we fear is real to us and
be patient with yourself as you are with a puppy dog.

May you walk the Earth in this body; feel
the bumps and bends, the curves and the swerves.

May you see the brambles and blind spots and self-
made booby traps.

May you recognise that all of this belongs to the
landscape of your life; it is not a definition of
who you are.

May each and every step, no matter how small, or
difficult, be in the direction of your own
true home.

May you hear your footsteps in the rhythmic da-dum,
da-dum, da-dum ...

...each and every one.

Blessed be the Face

I hold my face
in my two hands
like parental leaves
hold their freshly emerged bud,
firm and high
to the sky.

I feel their
gentle presence
like a prayer:

May this yet closed bud
open and grow
into the flower that it is.

I find myself
on my knees,
arms extended,
palms and face
to the sky.

And I receive
a blessing
for myself
and all beings:

May your face look out
at the world and offer
the flower within;
the flower that buds,
blossoms and dies

as does the moon
in its endless cycles
of waxing, waning
and disappearing;
as it is simply following
its own true face,
sunlit or not,
forever in tune with
the inevitable tides of oceans,
the undulating waves of breath
and life as it is here
on Earth;
life as it is
as earthlings.

Grace

High, I stand
she instills me

Fast, I write
she guides me

Low, I mourn
she meets me

Hard, I fall
she catches me

Deep, I sleep
she rests me

Patient, I wait
she reveres me

Fresh, I awake
she waters me

Round I swell,
she suns me

Pink, I blossom
she crowns me – queen of my nature.

Retreat

I am not blind.
I am not lost.
I am no longer a wretch:

I see
I am found -
I am here.

Para Doxa

We are human and also divine:
Divinity lifts us, takes us beyond
our limiting body
into the realm of angels.

We can fly in that realm!
We can fly in that realm!
And still stand solidly on Earth!
And still stand solidly on Earth!

We are divine and also human:
Humanity pulls us down
towards the earth
into the realm of Nature.

We can reside in that realm!
We can reside in that realm!
And still fly with angels!
And still fly with angels!

Bless the Children

I do not know what it is like
to be four and no longer able to walk,
no longer able to talk,
no longer able to play –
not due to a disease or disability,
but no food.

I do not know what it is like
to be in despair for years like you
who lost a daughter, then a son
aged one and three -
not due to a lack of doctors or hospitals,
but no more medicine.

I do not know what it is like
to be a soldier or a politician
or a victim of war and
I do not know what to do -
not due to inertia
but no more patience.

I do not know what it is like
to have no say, to be left to suffer
and starve whilst millions watch on
from the comfort of their homes –
not due to heartlessness,
but no more words.

I do know what it is like
to write poems that become
powerful prayers and blessings:

Dear children of Yemen,
you have not been forgotten.
I have seen
your gaunt eyes,
your twig-sized thighs,
your swollen bellies,
your facial expressions.

May your bellies be filled with food;
May your hospitals be filled with medicine;
May your generators not break down;
May the aid deliveries get through;
May you receive all the help you need;
May your bodies grow strong again;
May the laughter return and
May you be protected from any further
violence, abuse and neglect.

May you live in dignity
with joy,
with laughter,
with potential,
with rights
as all children have,
as all of mankind has,
- birthright -
that must
be returned.

Blind Navigation

I have heard that
some blind people
use sonar to navigate
through life
like bats.

I have been
visiting Anita
from the local farm.
I hardly know her
but for several years
have been to her shop,
bought meat and eggs,
milk, butter and cheese:
Tomini per la griglia,
Gorgonzola, Mozarella.

She is now in palliative care,
cannot walk or sit for
long, even in the wheelchair.

I dropped my dread
and other agendas,
dared to pay her a visit,
first in the farmhouse,
above the shop,
then in the hospice.

I did not know her,
I did not know
the right words in Italian;
how I may help,
what I might do
or how to be
with her.

I now trust
there truly is
a blind one inside
that can navigate
without being able
to see,
without knowing
how.

I listen to her stories,
stroke her hands.
Sometimes, when she cries,
I puff up the pillow,
make a cup
of Yogi Tea and we
list the spices we smell:
she, in Italian
I, in English.

Birds bring the
sound of spring
indoors and with them
the knowing: they are
building nests.

On Your Own Side

Be on your own side
of the wide river you are!
Be the turn in the curve,
the whirl by the rock,
and the beaver that leads
the way with her tail,
steering you back
to your own side.

One Key Fits All

Kindness is the key
that fits every human
heart - the one that turns
the internal lock –
even when rusty,
broken or clogged.

A simple word,
a gentle act
and the safe is cracked.

Compassion is the key
that fits our universal
heart - the one that turns
the eternal lock -
even when rusty,
broken or clogged.

A simple word-
a gentle act -
and we are in

the heart of all hearts:
divine humankind.

This Morning on the Rocky Ridge

I am becoming
intimate with the cloudless sky,
the still water of the lake
and the freshness
of this moment.

I am looking
at a new page
of my writing book,
noting down
the words I read
over and over
whilst in Plum Village[16] -
words that were written
on the walls and the doors;
words that were
hard to miss;
yet repeatedly
forgotten:

"I have arrived. I am home"

---

[16] Plum Village, near Bordeaux in southwest France, is the largest international
practice center in the Plum Village tradition, and the first monastic community
founded by Zen Master Thich Nhat Hanh (Thay) in the West.

New Year Advice I Like to Abide by

Rise early!
Walk through the woods at dawn,
or in the dark;
befriend mosquitos, spiders, dank places
and the mind
as it drives through all kinds of weather.

Set off each day for its own sake!
Love not knowing
why, or where you are going;
listen well to the whisperings
of the leaves,
of the trees.

Find a brook, or forest stream
and watch its waters run
towards lower ground.
Go swimming there
and let yourself be taken
to humble places!

Forgive the rocks for tripping you up,
the whirlpools and eddies
for turning you around
and the currents for taking you
where you do not wish to go.

Ride, glide and dive deep
without holding on -
even to your breath.

Hand-in-hand with yourself,
fall over this waterfall
and that waterfall.

Remember to surface for air!
You are human after all
and drowning is possible,
as is waking each morning
to a walk in the woods
and a dip in
all this sacredness.

Memo: remember to remember

Rest now, no haste now!
Stop here where you are!

Feel the warmth in your hand,
the beat in your chest,
the hairs in your nose
and your ears

returning you
here.

Hear the pulse that will not cease;
the drum and beat that speak:
remember to remember
you cannot fail at being
(or at breathing)

whilst you are living.

This is life's blessing
and we are all
already blessed.

Instructions for a Whole Heart

In our temporary home
on this floating rock
we call Earth,
stray from the path!

Follow the frog to the pool,
the bee to the bloom
and plunge childlike
into every rainbow!

Care for the person
you are - and go fishing,
not for compliments,
or with bait,
but for that slippery fish:
the one inside, the one
calling you
by your true name.

Remember: you are

Intrinsic intelligence,
depth of beauty,
immeasurable being -

Ours is a vast
and exquisite
walk on this earth.

Choose Love?

What really matters? What matters, really?
That you get lost in crossness, stress;
disliking this, dismissing that,
unable to stop or get out
of your way, caught in flight
or fight, and far from a sense
that life is just right as it is
and you are too?

What really matters? What matters, really?
That you hate all you see?
That you manage to judge
all aspects of 'me'?
That you are strewn every which way,
beside yourself anew,
crying:
what to do?
What to do?

What really matters? What matters, really?
That you choose kindness?
That you allow yourself,
this once, to just try
and do your best
at simply being 'yourself',
no matter what?

What really matters? What matters, really?
That you remember it's ok
if you contract into a ball;
into a space so tight and so small

that you feel alone and miles from home,
uncaring towards your humanness
with no desire to be 'yourself'?

What really matters? What matters, really?
Choosing love, above everything?
Remembering that you can 'be love', and 'be loving'
in very small ways, even in the midst of rage?
Even in the midst of shame and hate
and everything that makes you want to blame
yourself, or 'them'?

What really matters? What matters, really?
Choosing love, above everything?
Really?
Everything?
Giving yourself a hug in the midst of your sobs?
Saying 'Thank you for being you', no matter what?
Remembering something that makes you cry
till you laugh? Till you cry out in pain?
Till your insides are sore and your diaphragm is taut?
Till it's pressing down on your heart and guts?
Much too hard, much too hard!
And you simply cannot hold back any more:
Now that you have started, you have to go on and on
and you do with a parp, parp, parp
and then on to the big fat FART.

And your heart bursts open wide, wide, wide.
Mind stops still and decides, at last,
to choose love
above everything.

Advice for a Spiritual Warrior

Stop. Listen. Meditate.
Allow yourself to meet this state
of mind and do your best to be 'just kind'
to all you feel: those sorrows,
the painful shames, the throb in the jaw
and all the rage -
those moments of dread,
hot and wild in your head
and all the twisted thoughts,
the insane claims.

It is hard to stop, stay and listen
to what's going on - resistance is strong
as is the judging voice that wrongs your softness
and compassion for yourself.
All it wants is war and to be right,
once and for all to rule and throw
you off the path you walk steadily on.

Pleading will not help, nor will acting
out mind's pleas to flee. Trust yourself,
remember your vow:

*I am willing even where I am unwilling to let the
willingness come through.*

Willingness will come, determination, too.
Just bring friendliness along, the non-
judgmental one; the one who does not forget to
call this 'work', 'courageous' and of a 'strong and
a brave heart'; the one whose sole desire
is to create peace in the world.

On This Path

I have asked many questions;
I have headed in many directions;
I have eagerly searched for answers,
for methods and formulas,
for help from teachers and had
high expectations.

Now I am retiring; I am quitting,
simply stopping – and starting
to receive what my cells
have been teaching:

Be still and see
yourself being yourself;
yourself becoming what you already are
and be with what is here, no matter what.

Not even your cells
know
how many breaths
you have left.

Into Your Element...

... be the swan,
glide into your element!
Allow yourself to be
at home in the world!

Awkwardly you waddle on land;
effortlessly you swim in water;
gracefully you fly
(or glide) through the air.

The Question is Not

The question is not: how long will I live?
But, will I let experience in?

The question is not: can my heart open?
But, will it open again and again?

The question is not: what is my purpose in life?
But, will I move in the direction of my heart?

The question is not: who am I?
But, will I accept the gift:
the elixir of life itself?

Breathing Room

Mind half closed and drooping
after a sleepless night,
I wake feeling like wildflowers
that have been plucked
and put in a vase to perish.

I know I must swing those flaccid stems
over the edge of the bed,
let them fall to the floor,
connect with solid ground,
grow fleshy and long
and pull themselves
root-like towards Earth.

Miraculously, I am moved
along floors,
through doors,
down steps
and corridors
to the breathing room.

I turn the handle
I enter the space
I am received
I am breathed
I am opened
and returned
to my true place

together with the wildflowers
in the deep silence of the forest.

Morning Mantras

Stop. Wait. Listen.
I will call your name

Stop. Wait. Be still.
I will come to you

Stop. Wait. Receive.
I will fill your heart

Stop. Wait. Let Go.
I will take you there

Stop. Wait. Have faith.
I know where to go

Stop. Wait. Trust.
I reveal all to you.

Trusty Compass

Who says it is your task
to question why
you have been made
the way you have been made?

To find fault
in all that I do
and the ways
I stumble and fall?

I relate to you,
you relate to me
and hear you speak
many uncomfortable truths.

Open your hands
and take the invitation
we extend - say,

Yes, I do
and let yourself be:
just this way,
just this one.

And trust
that you, I, we
are all pointing
in the right direction.

Here with Me

You were with me today,
a hand on each shoulder,
pushing down – a steady pressure
not unlike stress;
yet a calm flow
bestowing upon me
a little poetry.

Time came and went again.
You came and went again,

leaving me
wondering whether anything
had been here
at all.

It felt unreal;
yet this page
is not
it is
here with me.

POEMS FOR WRITERS

The Delivery Room

We come to the delivery room
not even knowing we are
pregnant or that these contractions
are the real thing:
they are opening
up the canal,
pushing pumpkin
through.

I arrive alone
and soon, you are there too,
assisting the birth,
first as midwife
then as expectant mum
and the labour pains are shared
as is the work.

We never know
whether there is
just one or more
on the way
but our bundles of joy
do arrive and land
in open arms.

We sigh, we embrace, we give thanks -
to all midwives
to all mums
to all writers
who have ever delivered.

Serious Advice for Unformed Poets

Don't write poems for competition's sake!
Don't race to win!
Don't chase recognition!

Spend time instead at brook's tender edge!
Watch her splutter, barely a trickle!
Lean in like bamboo at her side:
stay and sway,
stay and sway!

Yes, stay and sway
in poetry time,
in time that flows
to and fro;
in time that circles
round and around.

Lean in, imagine
her under your skin;
how she moves silt,
wears down rock,
creates grooves and shapes:
deeper and deeper,
wider and wider,
on and on.

Let her spill
into your heart,
into your veins,
out of your hands,
onto the page.

It is pure play,
not a game –
a serious matter:
life or death!

Poems choose you, you know:
they want to be confirmed
and, in turn, they confirm you,
Poet.

What to Remember Each Morning

❖Ease body out of bed with care and intention.

❖Invite gratitude and kindness into the bathroom.

❖Let resistance and worry sit with a 'to do' list outside.

❖Wash the sleep from the corner of your mind.

❖Brush night's knots out of your heart.

❖Rub all dead things off your skin and let the light of day in.

❖Dress in multilayers, for all kinds of journeys on land, at sea, and in the air.

❖Don't forget the dash of 'Pleasures' scent!

❖And don your poet hat - that plumed one that makes you look daft.

❖Shoo away all poem-sucking insects like the *Blockquito, WordWorm, Page Lice, Ink Flee* and *Book Bug*.

NB: If all fails, tickle yourself in front of the mirror and have a good old giggle!

Before the Poetry Reading

Like a punctured rubber dinghy, my being crumples and folds, then sinks to the bottom of my murky mind. Lungs gasp for breath and ribcage clasps my tender heart to keep it from harm. Thoughts turn into a medusa – each tentacle tipped with all the reasons why I am not a poet and why I must not share my work. One glimpse and heart turns to stone, brain to sponge and stomach begins rotating backwards. I hear my own desperate cry from the deep: *I refuse to feel this! Not this!* And the doggy-paddling starts, head desperate to stay up, desperate to find a lifesaving device. A buoyant voice gets through the crosscurrents: *This moment has arrived as a gift - an invitation to truly feel what is here to feel – you can trust that all is well and let go of wishing things were different. Your guests will arrive - they are not your foes - you can ask them into your home, you share the same soul.*

Poet in Residence

It is decided!
From this moment on,
I am officially 'Poet in Residence'.
A contract – 'indefinite duration'
has been signed by me:
'The Poet'.

Whoever would have thought?
This 'Nobody' in the world of poetry;
a no one with no prize to her name,
has been given 'Permission
to write
poems all day –
on the premises or off.'

There is talk of a grant and
visits to all kinds of places,
towns, gardens, famous houses.

And it is all up to me, The Poet!

So, Poet in Residence,
the most sought-after post
in the world of poets,
what do you say?

I say: *this is my home;*
this is where I write;
this is where I am, Poet in Residence:
here in my garden, in the forest, by the lake,
by my sick mother's side,

on my bicycle,
at the shops,
at work and at play...

Now that I am Poet in Residence,
my heart gladly beats 24/7
and I am filled by a magical cup
that re-fills and re-fills;
words gurgling with the brook,
pouring into the lake:
Lago Maggiore -the major one – a deep
place and key:
a benediction of the beloved
ephemeral inside
and shapeshifting my chest,
my heart and hand,
word after word
inhale – exhale
inspiration – expression.

We breathe in unison.
Now,
in residence.

What is a Poem?

What is a poem?
What is sacred or real?
Could it be the heart of a moment?
The beat or brief pause between?
That split-second we hardly feel
as our in-breath turns to leave?

Sometimes, I perceive an interlude,
a space;
a rare instance of grace
as my mind slows down
and takes a
break.

Here,
I enter
in and briefly glimpse
as if through rapid eyelid blinks,
a breath
fanning my face
like the flutter of
a fruit fly's wing.

Can we understand this tiny thing?
Or that there are moments in which life is full,
complete and vast, despite knowing it will not
last?

Can we grasp that this fragile thing
is showing us
everything we need to know?

Can we believe this to be,
simple and plain

poetry?

Poem Falls

"Good morning rain!
What a lot you have to say -
tumbling down in silvery strings,
parachuting all from up there
down here to Earth."

A seasonal downpour
on a lawn; lushing the grass
(*Ah, music to a poet's voice*;
lyre to a psalm) and
my pen is poised to receive
all the sounds and tones of
shining poems...

Pen catches something more -
overtones never heard before;
ancient and ageless constellations,
suns and stars
and orchestrations...

I hear something falling
into water –
A sacred stone?
A healing crystal?

I hear something opening -
A scroll?
An oracle?
...

...I read:

You are not here
to find happiness.
You are here to wake up,
and rejoice in this
human experience.

Recognise the great work
mind has done

and remember only this:

who you really are.

Divine Force Shapes

Divine force shapes,
reveals our nature
like a sculptor reveals
shapes in a stone.

I am a poet in progress;
these poems take shape
as I progress
and reveal
who we are.

Poetry Time

You are a toddler
playing the same game
over and over,
kaleidoscope in hand
turning, turning, turning.

        Gazing through your eyes,
        I see over and beyond
        horizons
        into wider and wider
        circles

        and a space,
        still
        as the eye of a storm;
        as the inside of a bubble
        blown through a ring:
        a rainbow,
        a globe,
        whole universes:
        in one
        hand.

Poet in Residence Life

I want to talk about
the poet-in-residence
life; what it means
being here rather than there;
at home rather than away;
mindful rather than mind full;
opening and letting in fresh air
even in the midst of the urge
to shut all windows and doors.

I want to talk about
the curiosity that comes
alive; what it means
being present rather than absent,
full of compassion and a passion
for this place, this very moment;
holding still, looking and listening
even in the midst of the urge
to run far away from home.

I want to talk about
the awkwardness
inside; what it means
being in confusion and darkness,
lost in shyness, embarrassment,
shame and humiliation;
yet, even in the midst of the urge
to leave this body, this Earth,
to take the pen and begin to write.

Another Writing Book

Another writing book: blank sheets
entice and invite to play
in fields of unmarked snow.

Children take my hands;
we skip along - hearts first,
heads following with glee.

Here and there, now and then,
open-mouthed, arms and palms
wide too, we catch the falling flakes

and swallow before they melt.
All is refreshed inside and
pen jumps in, begins to write.

Usually it's a Tuesday

Around a table next to a fire,
food and wine to share with some words,
some conversation and sometimes,
poems.

We sit up close
and talk about
what we see,
what we feel
and whatever thoughts
come through.

This is not profound,
philosophical or with any pull
or purpose for everyday
life on planet Earth -
but dipping in
and out of poetry,
passion, vulnerability,
intimacy,
we word smiths,
speak, radiate,
weave,
sometimes well,
sometimes not,
but in this small group of poets,
worlds come together
and we sip.

Usually it's a Tuesday.

I Cannot Hold Back

I cannot hold back -
and there is no way back!

I have tumbled in
as I did at sixteen
into my first kiss
with the exchange boy from France
on the way back to my house.

I have no will to pull away
like that tongue that
plunged in
hot and unexpected
jump-starting my senses,
unplugging my heels,
lifting my spirit
off the earth.

My mouth,
your mouth
wide open, yet sealed together
in this new place -

Poems -
and terrifying
aliveness.

Twinkle in Your Eye

My mother never said
I was brought by Stork
(or by Swan, in fact)
but as 'a twinkle in her eye'.

This I believe to be true.
I grew inside her womb,
entrusted to her: a care-giver and
also a care-taker, each of us there
to bring the other alive.

"Who are you, Poem?" I ask.

A child of the stars.
A twinkle in your eye.
I wait for you
to be touched by beauty.

Look at tonight's sky!
See the intricate
patterns of light?

I gaze down at my newborn.
"Welcome," I say,
"I will take care of you.
Thank you for taking care of me."

Sometimes and Then... All is Resonance

I scare myself and others sometimes
extending or accepting invitations -
making promises to passions,
to participating in projects,
to saying 'yes' to possibilities,
to hearts opening widely,
to challenges and extremities,
to intensity and creativity
and to listening to my heart
speaking clearly and directly
and to only saying 'no' to
things that are not resonating.

I excite myself and others sometimes
like a bell that dings, a sweet *Tinkerbell*
or dongs a deep and loud *Big Ben*
the pen a divining rod
over these pages,
sourcing and finding
poems in the paper.
I hear hearts racing,
pounding and booming
like thunderclouds banging or
fluttering and quickening -
like butterfly wings beating
through airwaves and resounding
in and all around us.

I imagine myself and others sometimes
taking seats in orchestral pits,
taking our stands, our scores,

lifting a mouthpiece to our lips,
a bow to our strings,
sticks to our drums and beginning:
the brushing, the plucking,
the blowing and the piping,
the trumpeting and the drumming -
breaths ever-breathing,
hearts ever-beating,
all our bodies leaning,
swaying and working,
moving in circles into rhythms
and spirals radiating outwards,
rippling and joining -
entwining and entangling.

First, I may be prompting,
prompting, not responding -
then I may be responding,
responding and you are prompting;
responding, prompting,
prompting, responding;
and then we are entering,
joining and vibrating,
ringing and singing,
more of us tuning,
turning and playing,
crescendoing into being
callings and openings,
silence and symmetry-
all is
resonance.

Morning Writing Practice

I feel the tug of the tide, and
am hauled back
into the boat –
the boat that has no oars;
the boat I cannot steer;
the boat that rises and falls, then rocks or lolls
as it meanders its way to sea.

It is a boat for one and
I sit in it alone.

The wake shakes my brackish veins and
makes me pick up the pen –
the pen that contains ink;
the pen that can steer itself;
the pen that presses a nib to paper, then heads
into the blankness.

It is a line for one and
I jump into the sea.

Then, it is simple:
as simple as opening the garden hose,
water pouring out until the flower bed
is soaked;

as simple as a cloud floats,
fills, then spills its load;

as simple as a word forms in your head,
then comes out through your mouth;

as simple as a diviner picks up her rod;
a violinist, her bow;

as simple as
a child laughing out loud.

Intent

I am intent
on writing,
on seeing beauty,
on recognising aliveness,
on living this unique gift.

I take dictation and intuit
that my work will be published,
that I will become an established author:
'authorised' by society.

I notice this desire for fame,
for recognition and intuit:
it is a writer's feather tickling
the ego. I can laugh and carry on,
intent on writing,
intent on joining my tribe,
intent on returning to my true home:
authentic author.

We can create
a world of greater dimension,
a world beyond narrow thought,
a world in which self-centeredness is
a world of one source.

I do not claim to know the way
but am intent on offering
these feathered words (tickling my fancy)
and, hopefully,
other's too.

I Dip In

I dip in, away from May's drizzle, into a steaming bath. The sound of the waves I create echo across the freshly-tiled walls. Candlelight jumps a flickering yellow dance across the ceiling and I can suddenly smell the sand of Corsica's beaches, hear the breaking of waves. I am swimming in one of many secret lagoons behind wind-eroded cliffs. Water laps over me, licks lovingly at my wounds and I sink into the bliss of it. Silence seduces me and her thick flowing gown wraps around my skin, engulfs my face and seeps slowly in. Soothing, soothing, soothing. Simply, she lays me on her soft sea bed and loves me like only a soul sister can. She stays by my side as I sink, sink, sink to the bottom of this seemingly bottomless place. At first light, I surface, say goodbye and begin to write.

No Midsummer Day's Breeze

It was noted in June at the annual fair
where would-be poets were selling their wares
that the absence of a midsummer breeze
had the poor writers on their knees.

And when a customer voiced the request:
"A verse on breezes with plenty of zest!"
Too thick was the summer air
from which to pluck original flair.

And so home the poet took the task
hopeful that her muse would bask
in breezy days of inspiration,
rhythmic quirk and innovation.

Alas in the computer room,
no breezes came to fluff her plume;
it lay there idle on the keys
with notepad, mouse and some cheese.

Yes, cheese! And the magical mouse
came to life in the silent house,
nibbled at the food and started to speak
in specially-coded rhyming squeaks.

And the plume could suddenly write
without her hand (but only at night)
translating the many mouse-squeaked words
into line upon line of rhythmic verse.

You may not think this story is true,
but the mouse (who really was a shrew)
did tell the plume what to write
and ended this poor poet's plight

So now on days without a breeze,
you'll catch her falling to her knees
in front of mouse, plume and cheese,
begging for poetry – "Pretty please!"

Catcher of the Prose

When spring dew seeps sap into roots
and buds blush pink on the cherry,
the toddling grass trips up new shoots
and paints a lawn yellow-merry.

Dandelion dance frolics the night,
uncurling fresh stems to the dawn.
My fountain pen drinks of this sight
quenches word thirst through its straw.

Bubbling ink makes babble the brook
while peppermint peeps through the sage,
and sharp on the nib, something hooks,
fluttering fanned fins to my page.

A magical fish has been caught,
talk happy and brimming with time;
slapping a rhythm to my thoughts
and splashing them over with rhyme.

The fish gives me some violet scales
which he says I must try and cook
and flapping with a jumpy tail
back lands in the babbling brook.

Into a pot the scales I chase,
with wild sage, rosemary and thyme,
cook bubble a stew of sound taste,
into which my fountain pen dives.

The dish excites my writing leaf
makes tangy like lemon does balm;
I dine and feast on this new treat:
choice-morsels well reaped from the yarn.

Phrases grace-dance out of the pot
crash-sounding with oceanic roar,
spill writing fresh and fizzling hot
on the virgin page of this shore;

not thin verse or limp poetry,
not frothy chit-chat for to cheer,
but magnanimous moods of sea,
full of soul, dark secrets and fear.

Days long and nights this food I use
to season and baste this mint prose
and a story to spur my muse,
fair beauty in form and shape grows.

Long-spraying are my days and nights,
plunge happy and sprinkled with glee;
no other ships or rocks in sight
turn-tiding word-flowing for me.

A week goes by, a month, a year;
no ebbing can falter sure flow:
the violet scales, forever here,
in a book of poems to show.

Alas, one day, I sit pen-poised,
as my feast-tide flounders and turns.
The special stew, no longer moist
sticks hard to the bottom and burns.

My ink thick and blackened to tar
glues hasty my fountain pen closed
and a looming storm from afar,
at my carelessness whips and blows.

My mind flicks at the fishy words
till limp-finned in meaning and rhyme;
and into the water them herds,
like farmers must slaughter their swine.

Away from my sharp pen they swim
to that never-never word land,
where all rivers fill to the brim
with text from my mind-driven hand.

And there they multiply with zeal
into crooked and scaly lumps,
kick-bashing my good writer's meal
into ugly, monster-size clumps.

Weed-tangled, my sweet, sweet word-life
dry-bleeds all its ink, black and blue.
My lid shuts in creative strife
and those fish from the brook, I shoo.

Grey-washed ashore my writer mourns
like April cries tree-blossoms loose;
writing life, by that wise fish sworn
now sentenced to death by a noose.

A noose made by knots of the mind
twist-tying her writer down cruel,
verdict: GUILTY– an easy find:
joyously reaping from the pool.

POEMS PLAY AND SHAPE

Wish upon a Star...

... Pen offers herself,
drumstick to my page -
and blasts, and backbeats
and bo-diddleys
my spirit's
boom-whackers.

In this Garden

I am withy
rollicking
the Poa Tree

Friend Osier Withe
and I
braid rose-
merry with time,
loosen Mistle's hold
on our toes,
fan our fares
to the sky.

Germitaleng I[17]

O notti of March
you scintillate breit:
star Spritz and super luna -
voll, piena,
completa -

You and I
Du and Ich
insieme -
inside
this bright moon.

---

[17] Germitaleng: marriage of German, Italian and English.

Translations: notti (Italian): nights; scintillate (English and Italian): to twinkle, sparkle; breit (German): wide (pronounced 'bright' and it can also mean drunk); Spritz (German): a splash or squirt (widely used to refer to the aperitif 'Spritz' - a liqueur based drink with a 'splash' or 'squirt' of prosecco; luna (Italian): moon; voll (German): full; piena (Italian): full; completa (Italian): complete or full; Du and Ich (German): you and I; insieme (Italian): together (adverb) or whole (noun).

Germitaleng II[18]

Star zitter
spring-born Wunder:
primavera and
spirit of grappa,
gripping like ferro,
stark and full
of sorpresa
like Waldmeister
- master of the woods -
creeping along
the understory,
light footed,
starry faces shivering
white and verde,
fabelhaft
bellezza
like us
masters
of these woods.

---

[18] Germitaleng: marriage of German, Italian and English.

Translations: German: zitter (tremble); Wunder (wonder); Waldmeister (literally master of the woods, it is the name given to the plant woodruff or gallium odoratum); fabelhaft (splendid, fabulous). Italian: primavera (spring); ferro (iron); sorpresa (surprise); verde (green); bellezza (beauty).

Bedtime in Luxembourg

I never really understood
When my mother said:
Be sure to wash your *féiss*[19]
before you go to bed.

Here is a face cloth,
here is a brush,
so brush your teeth
and wash your *féiss*
and into bed you race.

A face cloth for a foot wash?
How very bizarre!
That's bedtime in Luxembourg -
Tra la la la la
That's bedtime in Luxembourg -
Tra la la la la.

[19] The Luxembourgish word *féiss* is pronounced like face and means feet.

Fouling around the Fruit Bowl

I may be a granny, all wrinkly and have a wee bit of
'grangreen', but who'll look after the sour grapes
when I'm gone?

Mouldy? Me, mouldy? - that green furry bit is my
winter bobble hat thank you very much!
It was a present from no other than
Mr Del Monte himself!

Rotten? Calling me rotten are you? Aging beauty more
like! If I go, then so do those pathetic kiwis.
Not only are they greener, they're also hairier.

As for you, bananas,
if it weren't for me, you would never ripen!

Why all this fussing and foul language?
No fruit bowl should be without the rotten apple!

Besides, who will pay you any attention
when I'm gone?

Strictly for the Birds

Ape was beavering away with Badger, which bugged Buffoon and so he decided, buffoon that he was, to ferret out Rabbit and together with Chicken, ape and badger them and fox them once and for all. Rabbit was chicken and Chicken could only rabbit on about what a buffoon Buffoon was, so before they could fox Ape and Badger, the eager beavers had managed to swan in, get the ferrets on their side, dog Rabbit, Chicken and Baffoon, buffalo everyone, and swan off!

In the Place I am Now

In the place I am now
Life = Love. I am
loving the sound, smell, taste, even of burps and farts
and the 'cumbersome me' in me, in others,
in relatives, friends, close family and not.

In the place I am now
Dead = Alive. I feel
life pulsing everywhere, in everything, even in the dying,
diseased and the dark, 'gruesome me' in me, in others,
in relatives, friends, close family and not.

In the place I am now
Fear = Joy. I am not afraid
of all that there is in this moment, even of things unwelcome,
bad, ugly, and the 'awesome me' in me, in others,
in relatives, friends, close family and not.

In the place I am now
Death = Birth. I inter am
says Tich Nhat Hanh: no death of anything, even of the dead,
the alive and forgotten 'loathsome me' in me, in others,
in relatives, in friends, close family and not.

In this place I can call home
Feeling = Believing. I skip along
with all that's present, even with pain, loss, tears and
the untransformed 'me' in me, in others,
in relatives, in friends, close family and not.

In this book in which I write
Poet + Poem = Poetry. We dance
together inside the paper, inter-being
with the tree that once stood in the forest;
with the cloud that once rained down to earth;
with the squirrel that once leaped through branches;
with the lumberjack that loaded the lorry full of timber;
with the book binder, the shop keeper and the Me in 'me'
with the I in You, the We in Us: the divine and human in All.

Anticipating the Call

I sit still
   in that strange territory:
       no plan,
       no strategy,
       no knowledge of outcome –

Wild

     like an elephant
        on
      groundless

       ground

      a bl

          b
         of
        mercury
        sus-
        pend-
         ed
         in
         st
       my ery.

Back Together

creativity

take   and

will   p

I   o

ur

like

cream

all over

my wounds;

crevasses will

fill and mix with

the grit inside, gluing

all-lost-pieces-and-fragments

c r e a t i v e l y rehtegot kcab

Water Borne

Are
we not
all droplets,
swimming away
from sirens - to land,
hoping we will be safe,
or singled out - the one
and only special
and unique
one?

We
yearn
to grasp
who we are,
why we are here
& wish to just relax
into the truth of it all.
Yet, undergirding our
swell, there really is
no solid ground –
and we do not
want this
to be
true.
Do
we not
know we are
falling like tears
fall into one another,
bound to merge with
everyone, and every
thing and there is
no single way
through
this?

Mindful Moment

I am
a fresh flower,
a solid mountain
a deep-rooted tree,
wild and still water;
I am fully here and
feel the fullness
of this that
I am.

Dressing in Blessing

I centre myself in
spirit, ground myself
in gratitude: may   I trust in the mystery
          of life may I love myself deeply and completely,
may I know what I want
                and be decisive;
      may I feel vibrant, hopeful
                      and fully alive,
  and step forwards with confidence,
            taking great care   of my heart, honouring
my inner warrior;
              may I assert myself
          peacefully,
                  let go of judgements
                easily and may,
                    I be
                    kind
            I centre   ♡   myself in
      spirit & ground myself in gratitude:
I breathe in fresh air & inspiration, breathe
out stale air & regret; I release guilt, fear anger
& shame, and live fully in the now. In the now
nourish myself with love, nourish myself with
    love nourish myself with love, nourish my-
      self with love, nourish myself with love.
      And now I enter into this new day;
          with a compassionate heart,
            a confident body, and
              a mind grateful,
                and filled
                up with
                spirit
                  x

1: One Company

Me
being
the only
one here, I pick
myself for the job of
Chief Executive Officer,
C.E.O of
1: One
to run a
business :
"Being Here"
vowing to pay
in gold, all those
who pick themselves.

Wholly Communion

I write, therefore I am.
I live, therefore I write.
I die, therefore I write.
I write before I die,
and live this life
fully & alive
Amen
I
I
I
I
I
I
I
I
amamamamamam

SONNETS

Sonnet I

Shall my first sonnet grant you some courage?
And praise mine and your vulnerable hearts?
As hardy a heart must grow and flourish;
it must grow tender; must grow wide apart;
and doubt grow in, like bindweed twist around;
and buds, shoots and all things fragile and new
rip, and fall off their stems, to newer ground;
and you too must fall, soft-sapped through and
through;
yet, doubt not your heart - vibrant - it will grow
in gardens you do not try hard to tame.
O dandelion so ripe! O wind that blows!
Such poems will find you over and again.

Let it be known, heartbind does not exist!
Trust not your mind! Poetry will persist!

Sonnet II

My man, my husband, my stark German oak,
you have dug deep my loam, my fertile soil
and rooted down into my depths: bespoke?
Well-branched and sturdy in love as in toil,
your wide trunk braced for every sort of storm:
all the booms, bolts and cracks of married life -
yet when turned willowy and limp in form,
I hung low, weeping, melancholic wife -
your rough bark offered neither warmth nor hold;
I slipped downunder where worms and moles hide,
learned to dig tunnels through nights dank and cold.
Forlorn, yet not lost: those roots were my guide.

They say of trees: as above, so below;
of our love, I say: it is true! I know.

Sonnet III

The poetry grows lush inside these woods,
on duffs, in brooks and all around the trees.
How merrily I'd dwell here if I could;
I'd while my days with Zephyr strumming leaves
and singing songs of chestnut, oak and pine;
of ferns, of birds and earthworms, praising you:
San Quirico[20] a realm of sense and rhyme,
where jay is jay and I to I am true;
yet home is home, I know I must return
for I belong among the human kind;
your magic essence bright inside - it burns
with luminosity beyond the mind:

O woods on Earth, your charm is plain sublime
and Zephyr too - enchantment is divine!

---

[20] San Quirico is the name of a chapel and the woods surrounding it. It is on a hilltop along the shore of Lago Maggiore in the province of Varese, Italy

Sonnet IV

This sacred place is not inside that church,
nor high atop the soaring purple bluff;
but far beyond where stands of silver birch
let catkins prance with playful poplar puffs;
their tops aloft, they hail and lead the breeze
across a sky alight with golden dust;
infused, the trees shake shimmies into leaves,
and tinkle bells of promise, zeal and trust;
yet only bards will lean against their trunks,
and dip their hearts and quills in tender swoon;
to drink Betula sap until most drunk,
then sing aloud their wisdom songs and tunes:

O Lady of the Woods let's bow to you,
and chant the words and verse that are your due.

Sonnet V

"Hello, dear Willow, childhood friend, hello!
How well you taught me through your gentle play;
your swinging game - *Oh let's sway to and fro
and swish and whoosh each joyful, lively day!"*
My arms entwined with yours, we wove our rope
and swung up high, to: *higher than the stars!*
"Remember this? My glee? My childlike hope?
The promise: *Keep this moment ever ours!"*
I've wandered far abroad and from your side;
my bond with you, at times, I sheer forgot;
yet vows, like roots, grow broad and firm and wide;
and haul us back to every cherished spot.

Each day you wave and bow by water's edge,
reminding me to cite my timeless pledge.

Sonnet VI

Do humans have the freedom to decide
their path, their purpose and the way to love?
Does heaven live inside or high above
the stars that shine as our eternal guide?
Is there a force by which we must abide?
Or laws and formulas for real truelove?
Is peace the only song we hear from doves?
And heart? Our home? Is this where truth resides?
I know not much but what I know I feel
as real as when our trowels dig in soil
and chop and smooth those clods without a break;
fine-grained, the ground invites us both to kneel:
We plant ourselves together: no recoil –
our rootstalks bond and knot for love's own sake.

Sonnet VII

Do scientists make peace by making bombs?
Do stars decide their constellated lines?
Can wisdom found in poems and in songs
align the universe for all of time?
Do mountain tops look up to outer space
where planets, suns and moons glance down to Earth
and hope this mind expands for every race,
grows spacious, vast and full, reveals our worth?
Such questions are too grand for one alone;
yet ask I must and trust they will be heard -
each one, a prayer that drops like many stones
and ripples out in circles, word for word.

May universal blessings be the way
beneath the way to beautiful array.

Sonnet VIII

O life, you hide and seek propinquity
and mystery, jump here and now with is-
ness, trump with packs of synchronicity,
coincidence and meaning full-ness, this-
ness; under-play arising like a wave;
a feral mare, unleashed, no bit, no rein;
but loose and I am surfer, I am brave;
no sense in charging, bailing, making tame
the foam, the decks; your horses peeling on
propelled by winds that surge, by stars and lore
of folk, of moon, of lots, of luck, of draw.
No matter how – I'm brought bespoke to shore.

Your deals, your ways, we'll never understand;
yet stand we can, and leap into your hands.

THIS IS NOT ABOUT POEMS

This is not about Butterflies

In some places,
one may imagine
'tis butterfly season.

Painted Lady
dances with Artemisia;
Admiral stands alone
on crumbling bracken.

Whilst some hungry caterpillars
nibble on winter green,
another of its kind
has metamorphosed
into spring

and found the perfect place
to lay her eggs.

This is not about Lizards

Lucertola! Lucertola![21]
spring light has called
and here you are,
free of your sluggish
winter home,
dancing in the sun.

---

[21] Lucertola is the Italian word for lizard. It contains the word 'luce' meaning light. The first rays of spring light lure lizards out from under the ground to search of food.

This is not about Thunder

I scare myself,
clapping out loud -
trumpeting:
Here I am!

I hear plant cells racing,
pounding and booming,
then fluttering and quickening, -
like butterfly wings beating.

I see Earth lifting
violin to her chin,
flute to her lips

as Rain and I
drum and drum and drum
in spring.

This is not about Leaves

Before I rake you,
I will count you.

I will count first in tens,
then tens of tens to a thousand,
then thousands of thousands.

I will touch each unique one of you
before I place you together
with all the other unique ones
onto the pile and
I will sculpt you
into a mountain.

All the while,
I will count.

It may take me a lifetime
for me to count -
for you all to be counted

I will count this lifetime,
then lifetime after lifetime
after, lifetimes after lifetimes.

All will be counted: each and every one,
till present,
each and every one.

This is not about Star Trek

Today, I was watching
Star Trek Discovery
from a half-beamed place of being,
barely visible,
barely an outline,
barely showing -
though I knew
I was made up
of zillions of particles,
and I knew,
just like here
in the movie theatre,
a place had been reserved
just for me.

And then, whilst watching,
I saw myself
beam through

and I stepped out
of the movie
into full technicolor.

This is not about Fennel

Fronds are often discarded,
but I save them for last;
for their promise of sweet anise
and for those feathers
that tickle my palate.

I chop the hollow stalks
clear off the bulb;
then snip, snip, snip -
off with all the wisps.

I slip them onto my tongue.
Oh, the thrill as they brush
my teeth with licorice!
And this hunger,
that was snoozing,
awakes.

This is not about Soup

No one eating my soup?
Full of goodness, florets of broccoli, hate and
bitterness?

No one eating my soup?
Taste and want not carrots, greens,
jealousy and rot?

No one eating my soup?
No-thanks family, courgettes, potato and
love in deficiency!

This is not about Coffee Tables

I visited a psychiatrist -
my appointment was today.
I waited with his coffee table -
it had a lot to say:

The Gun
Killing Fields and White Death
Indicted Killers
Exit, Stage Left
The Next Chernobyl
World at War
Tears and Terror in East Timor
The Sole Survivor
Food and Flight
Eyes on the Eclipse
Every Soul's Right.

This is not about Blackbird Song

Thumb and pointer poised
then let down to the page
like, during Beatle mania,
the needle to a vinyl.

A voice sounds
as if from nowhere;
nowhere that is somewhere
inside the grooves.

And blackbird song
arises
through the dimness,
loud and clear.

This is not about Cloaks

My girth is wide and I can
disguise, or swallow whole
daggers and knives.
I love to hang around
Count Dracula and I love
the power I have
to conceal,
make things disappear,
or stay hidden
whilst I pull strings
and other things
under cover...

...an ideal
place for a game
of hide and seek.

This is not about Engines

Bother me about mechanics
and how to care
for sumps,
for rings,
for cranked-up engines
and fine-tuned things.

Yes, please bother me
about slaps and knocks
of pistons and cogs, the sounds
of rusty old pumps;
things that go,
things that stop,
all that works
and all that
does not.

This is not about Herons

In the night, the north wind picked up
our satellite dish, flipped it on its back,
then set it back down a saucer-shaped cup.

For a week, we have seen heron dropping
in sticks and twigs and things.

Impossible! Herons don't nest on roofs!
Our friends said, as Heron landed
on the dish and settled in to lay her eggs.

This is not about Pumas

"Pumas have gone missing!" the local police
declared, "Beware of noises in
the early morning, behind houses,
under porches. Sightings have been made
between 3 and 5!

One puma has been caught on camera
in a tussle with a golden retriever.
The other is still AWOL in the neighbourhood.
If you see a sign, you are advised:

Check if it's male, size:
European 45,
then inform the police!"

This is not about Clocks

There are hands and fingers
that point and a voice
that counts, but there are no rounds
of sixty, twelve, twenty-four;
nor is there a hint of a sound
or a single tick tock, though
faces say: it is now morning,
                it is now evening
and light up
in the middle of a dark night,
become dim
in the middle of a bright day.

It cannot be stopped
or beaten, turned forward or
back, punched, rolled, killed or cleaned.
Despite what our mind says,
we have no other choice
but to follow fingers that point
beyond what we can comprehend;
beyond what appears to pass us by,
fly away, get lost or become dead -

Simply because
nothing else truly counts
or makes any sense.

This is not about Time

All these 'things to do'!
All these 'musts' that
must weave into a day;
things that insist on being
part of my life –
part of my purpose.

I say I want to dance alone
without partners
that are too short,
that breathe down my neck,
are too late, run out, or go missing.

I wonder –
if I spin around fast enough,
will I,
erase my beginning,
have no end?

I stop dancing now
and gaze at the clock.
I see it is time to go
to the post office
before it closes,
pick up the letter
from the bank -
the letter that contains
a new credit card.

Who knows?
This may be
the ticket –
give me more credit
than anything this world
could ever offer.

This is not about Beaches

Bare feet feeling
dark grains dancing;
waves lapping,
scrubbing and licking;
skin tingling,
flying and crying,
'curvy, all curvy',
like the gulls
all-a-circling
like shells
and pebbles;
salt-crystal fringes
- seams ever changing;
moist sand entering,
squeezing in creases;
nostrils streaming,
gaits leaping,
toes baking,
earth flashing,
pinkness shining
through
all the
blues.

This is not about Breezes

Zephyr, you appear!
You appear
to breeze
over years of dead leaves
then disappear
to the unseen deep
by a blown-down tree
and a still,
still stream.

This is not about Ladybirds

Tiny creature so bold,
flying this winter,
alighting as the moon
softens these stiff hotel sheets
with its brightness.

I am awake - no mistake -
you are no bothersome fly!
Oh, lucky beetle – welcome!
Share my pillow tonight!

Are we lying comfortably?
Then you may begin:
Lady of seven joys and sorrows,
tell me your true stories!

I wake early and you are
still here on my pillow –
I squeal, childlike
and we fly brighter
than moon's glow
from the rising sun.

This is not about Light

She'll get in
where nothing else does,
find her way
through pin holes,
hair wide cracks,
around bends, over blocks
and the walls you have built.

She'll get in.
She won't be stopped.
When she wants to break in,
bursting with speed,
she'll reach through
to where you squat
at the bottom
of that dark pit.

She'll get in,
seek you out,
drill her beams
into your head
into your being,
penetrate in
and let
your light
out.

This is not about Frida Kahlo and Diego Rivera

What I saw that day, beyond
our names and fame of our works; beyond
the turmoil, betrayal and pain
of our troubled bond; beyond
our passions and the tumultuous road
we were on; beyond
the personal, the public and
all of life's paradoxes....

What I felt that day: the possibility
of love between dove and elephant;
between the surreal and real;
the ephemeral and material.
My art - an expression of the intangible:
inward longing for belonging and connection.
His art – an obsession with the tangible;
outward faith in a social state
and industrialisation...

...despite what Frida said:
"Though I married, divorced,
married him once again
and each day saw love
unfold in and out of strife,
out of discord with the norm,
through storms of rage and power play,
drug-driven forays, mean behaviour,
inebriation and the cruel,
but natural ways
we were not our best

in this modern, Western world."
We went beyond.

That day,
I stepped in front of his portrait
(In Memory of Frida)
after I had gone,
lost forever as wife
from his physical side,
I found myself in a space,
connected once more to the hand
that stroked my face into being
and through the glass, I looked
and felt heat emanate as once
I had when painting
the flames in Flower of Life
and, though I was dead,
I swear,
Diego pulsed on
inside my chest.

This is not about Fact, but Meaning

Clay
/klei/
 n.
1. Picasso holds a clod of earth, moulds it into a jug (or a bowl) and a masterpiece is born: practical and affordable by all. He wrote Potter's Bible and told the story of how earth can be transformed into priceless art. Everyone who read it, drank (or ate) from such jugs (or bowls) and became rich (in more ways than one). Picasso could have saved us from greed, poverty (and war) but most of us didn't want to get our hands dirty.
2. When naked, his body and my body look the same from behind. No wonder, we were formed from the same raw material as are the twins in my womb. Now only the size of clods, they will become full (separate) bodies. Angel Gabriel flew by one day to say he will fill (and connect) them with Holy Spirit.
3. (Connected to all of above) colloq. *put that in your pipe and smoke it.*

This is not about Judgement, but Truth

Placing my hand square on the book,
I swear to tell
the truth...the truth...the truth.

"Where did you say
you came to be in possession
of this precious thing?"

"I found it on the leaf-littered path I take
through the woods.

Steal? I do not steal!

I feel each leaf underneath my feet.
I see words along the lines of their veins.

The woods are full of poems,
waiting for us to pick them up,
take them home."

AFTER POEMS
with reverent bows to the inspiring poets

The Mind and The Heart

After Edward Lear's, The Owl and the Pussy-Cat

I

The Mind and The Heart went to sea
    In a beautiful man-made boat,
Like two desperados, they carried bravado,
    Well braced so that all would float.
The Mind looked down at the waves below,
    And spoke his pure thoughts aloud,
"O lovely Heart, O Heart my beau,
    What a beautiful Heart art thou,
        Art thou,
        Art thou!
    What a beautiful Heart art thou!"

II

Heart said to The Mind, "You are one of a kind!
    How rhetorically well you speak!
O let us be One! else this journey be long:
    But how? Shall we find a technique?"
They sailed away for many a day,
    To the land where Spirit Man grows
And there in a wood a guru stood
    With a drum and chants set in prose,
        In prose,
        In prose,
    With a drum and chants set in prose.

III

"Dear Guru, may we take for peace-of-man's sake
    Your drum?" Said The Guru, "You may!"
So they took this one chance to drum into trance
    Till the night (black and thick) turned to day.
They danced in the light with much insight,
    Which delighted The Sun and The Moon;
And pace after pace, arms full of embrace,
    They continued in love and till noon,
        Till noon,
        Till noon,
They continued in love and till noon.

Greed and the Big Feed

After Benjamin Tabart's chant of the Giant in Jack and the Beanstalk.

Fee fi fo fum,
I smell the heart of a human one.
Be it right, or be it wrong,
I crave to feed his grabby tum.
That gobble sound – Oh how delish!
A gourmet sip of swinishness!
Hog-hog throats and gimmie eyes,
gripping limbs and gurgling minds.

Oh, how I'd love to lure one in:
a feast for two on deadly sin!

Thank You...I am: a writer's song

After and (roughly) to the tune of Thank You
by Alanis Morissette

I slip off the wings of love
for life's wonder.
I don't care when or if
I'll ever fly.
Inspiration comes and moves
swiftly through me: blown away
by my own critical mind.

Thank you, gratitude
Thank you, patience
Thank you, continuity
Thank you, faith in me
And love in me
And belief in who I am

I fall to the ground of
mind's narrow darkroom.
I feel nothing,
I'm no-one and no more.
Dreams, passions - everything
that used to move me -
sprawl limp and lifeless
all over the floor.

Thank you, gratitude
Thank you, patience
Thank you, continuity
Thank you, faith in me
And love in me
And belief in who I am

The moment I am vulnerable
Is the moment I am humbled
The moment I am humbled
Is the moment I am true.

I feel my spirits rise up
when I'm writing.
Pen moves hand and arm till
heart opens wide. I see I've grown wings
and they are opening,
giving me flight, lifting me back
into life.

Thank you, gratitude
Thank you, patience
Thank you, continuity
Thank you, faith in me
And love in me
And belief in who I am

Yeah, yeah
Oh, oh, oh
Oh, oh, oh
I believe in who I am.
I believe in who I am.

Ode to Rough Paper

After Odes by Sharon Olds and with a reverent bow to Dr Seuss

You are so rough and haptic, you trip up
my writing hand and rub the side of my pinkie
pinker. But forgive me, finger, you say, I am recycled
paper, as ethically un-chemical as man could muster,
paper with zero added -
0 ozone,
0 chlorine,
nothing foreign, just fresh and honest like
Odes by Sharon Olds.
I bought her book and am eating her words:
Ode to the Penis
Ode to the Clitoris
Ode to Buttermilk

I'm letting tongue linger, tasting those buds,
licking, lapping - nothing hasty –
wanting for nothing more, or less, not least a fast;
but to make this feast last longer than it would
if gulped down, or taken in intravenously.

(*Sorry to intervene here but I do hope this Olds diet
works and I will shed extra pounds: the weight of
words that hang around my jaw; the ones that push
themselves onto my tongue like onto a diving board;
the ones that bounce up and down, insist they must
be picked, insist they must have the first and last say.*)

But it's okay because, like you and like
Sharon Olds, I want words that are known,
yet surprise;
words that can mean many things as they join in lines
like, The Cat in the Hat
or Green Eggs and Ham...
...full of rhythm and rhyme,
easy to read and understand; yet words which change
ideas, tear things down that were stuck inside;
words that are so small and light they seem like
nothings: Thing One and Thing Two kind of words that
disturb the peace and
a mind that is against them;
a mind that wishes to follow rules,
go straight to the point and be organised;
a mind that insists it does not like
green eggs and ham from Sam I Am;
a mind that wants none of the messiness
Things One and Two make in the house
(though the cat cleans it up in the end).

And you lend yourself to the task.
You give me an Eaton Mess kind of messiness,
full of crunch, taste and well,
sense - like a toothbrush for our teeth
and beaker for the brush to keep it in its place,
stop it lapping up soap suds on the side
of the sink when you have left it lying there
with nothing to do until evening and it gets bored
waiting for its second performance. Such a long
interval, you can't blame a brush for getting involved,

licking it clean like it's a cake-mixing bowl,
or a lover's mouth, or a book of Sharon's Odes
(*as I have mentioned thrice in this poem*).

Ah, poem?
Poem, you say?
Nay, no, not, cannot be,
0 correct,
just scrap, scrapings,
no – the dregs
from a bored poet with too much time
between performances!

Yet here the poem stands
and this jaw, these hands
feel much lighter; pinkies are much, much pinker
and the other fingers are licking themselves
for making words work (hard) for a living
as they scraped over you,

O, my dear tough, rough paper
to which zero was added
but these scribbled lines,
now worth more to the poet
than anything in the world
with or without
0, or any number of
0s, in it.

Sonnet XVIII

After Shakespeare's Sonnet 18: Shall I Compare Thee to a Summer's Day

Shall I compare thee to a willow tree?
Thou art more lithe and more magnificent:
Rough winds strip catkins, singe leaves by degree,
And howl till bark is split, and bough is bent:
Sometime too cracked a sallow comes to ground,
And often is that wildwood grandeur lost;
And many babylonica de-crowned
By gardener's sharpened secateurs, or frost;
But thy aliveness never will be trimmed
Nor lose the pinnacle that's truly thine;
Nor shall thy effervescence e'er be dimmed,
When seeds of bards gestate within thy mind:

So long as genius breathes with grace abound,
So long lives thee by aspiration crowned.

There's a Wook in my Book

After Dr. Seuss 'There's a Wocket in my Pocket'.

Sometimes I have to find it:
the humour in the rumour,
the treasure in the pressure
and the fun in the pun.

When my mind is not being kind
and the thoughts have me caught,
I need to do such deeds
as find the laugh in the bath,
the bubble in the trouble
and the giggle in the wriggle.

But that's not so easy peasy
when your head is full of lead
and a rowdy voice is shouting
in that head that's full of lead.

How rotten! I had forgotten
there's a Wocket in my pocket
for those moments full of woments
when that judging is not budging
and the shirking is not working,

How easy now I see it,
The Wocket in my pocket
and with The Wocket in my pocket,
I can catch and snatch and tatch them:

The Wook in my book,
The Bover on my cover,
The Woems in my poems,
The Zages in my pages,
The Tinks in my ink and
The Wapters in my chapters.

Yes, there's a Wocket in my pocket
that can face and chase and wace them
with a giggle and a wiggle
and a sniggle
all the way.

ESSAYS AND PROSE

Under the Wisteria

I sit on the patio under the wisteria, or rather, a grey twisted vine that looks so thick and strong that it appears to be holding up the pagoda single-handed, when my attention is caught by a daffodil. It bobs its head as if agreeing with whatever its neighbours, crocus and anemone, are saying. Doves are getting on with nest building and I get on with writing. All is quiet except for the sound of the birds fluttering in and out of the pond, sipping, then pecking at moss in the lawn and picking up twigs for their new home. Behind me, the mimosa is a shock of yellow amid an otherwise dull and brown landscape and has attracted the attention of some bees.

All this life: plants and creatures being unutterably themselves whilst I sit here, unutterably not myself, not knowing what to do, not knowing when or if Dad will ever get out of hospital. He's been there for a week already, connected to a mass of tubes. I called and asked, 'How are you, Dad?' 'I'm alive,' he said, 'but not kicking much.' He was crying as he uttered this amended version of his usual, 'I'm alive and kicking!' I also cried after I hung up. I'm not ready for him to die. Are we ever ready?

I have just finished reading Sebastian Faulk's book, Human Traces. The closing words are really what the book was about:

"Human beings could live out their whole long life without ever knowing what sort of creatures they really were; perhaps it did not matter, perhaps what was important was to find serenity in not knowing."

I copy the quote down, underline: <u>*find serenity in not knowing*</u>, and vow to not let 'not knowing' drive me mad any more.

Pain, regret, loss – they are as much a part of life as are love, joy and passion. In the end, I live, I die and life goes on unfussed about who I am, how I experience it, or whether I have the foggiest idea what it is all about.

I may as well just accept that simply turning up and living my life, no matter what is going on, is most important.

And without dwelling on my question: *What is writing good for when my father is dying*? I simply write: *I don't know*! and suddenly feel unutterably at peace with the world.

Morning Pages

There is an English proverb:

Absence makes the heart grow fonder
or
Always toward absent lovers love's tide stronger grows.

(From the Elegies of Roman poet Sextus Propertius)

I re-open my writing book after some absence. It isn't that I haven't been writing, it is just that I have been writing a diary-like account of travels, events and happenings over the summer months rather than 'practicing' writing. By practicing, I mean writing whatever is on my mind, in my heart, in my dreams; whatever enters into the ink and flows out through my arm and hand and pen and onto the paper.

I now feel the tug of that tide, love's tide, and realise something surprisingly ordinary and at the same time, something that is urgently important: everything I have missed about this kind of writing equals all this practice gives me, daily. And I do indeed feel my heart stir again, growing not only fonder, but also full of awe for this practice. So for future reference, I thought it would be useful for me to write down all I missed:

- ❖ A moment of communion with myself exactly as I find myself.

- ❖ A moment of listening, hearing and daring to voice my innermost thoughts, desires and emotions.

- ❖ Simply turning up and allowing writing to come, sentences to form, thoughts to bubble up and manifest themselves from the depths.

- ❖ A place to 'put' all the 'stuff' that would otherwise swim around my head like goldfish, passing the same scenery over and over ad nauseum; the stuff that has the power to drag me into some dead and stagnant place and hold me captive there, captive in thought patterns and belief systems that are far from healthy or encouraging.

❖ Simply sitting here on a cold wooden stool at the kitchen counter, leaning over my writing book into the warm pool of light that shines down from above my head.

❖ The sensation of the side of my hand stroking the paper, the way I might stroke a hamster, the way a brook smooths roughness from stones.

❖ My writing instrument, snug between pointer, middle finger and thumb, ready and poised for the first movement, the first stirring, like a magician her magic wand; a diviner, her rod; a violinist, her bow.

❖ Gazing into the garden at dawn, greeting the waving branches and nodding back to them – Ah, yes, it is a windy start, or Oh, how calm it is after last night's storm, or we're in for a sprightly, playful morning, I see.

❖ Remembering all that is alive in me, however subtle or imperceptible.

❖ Trusting intuition – regardless the challenge - I can invite writing into that place and know I will receive guidance.

❖ Mining my bedrock and beyond through the underground into the places that are hidden and secret and scary.

❖ Alone time, time for being.

❖ All the poems that simply appear.

Shutters

My bedroom window has shutters. They are rolled up neat and tight around a metal pole in a box above it. A synthetic cord is attached to the inside wall so that I can let the shutters down, or pull them up.

On the outside, there is a gap between the window frame and the shutter box and this has enabled a pair of blue tits to get in and build a nest. For weeks, I have watched them come with moss, twigs and the like. Now they bring delicacies such as live caterpillars, flies and other bugs. I find it difficult to tell male and female apart. Both carry food in. I also have no idea how many baby birds are inside the shutter box. There could be up to fourteen, according to my bird book.

I cannot help but admire the birds' teamwork and dedication to the task of feeding their babies. I wonder whether the parents have time to feed themselves, or to rest. I conclude that they probably do it on the wing! It's not important for them right now. What's important is that the chicks receive nourishment and grow strong enough to leave the nest when the time comes.

When the shutters are up, light floods into my room and the birds can get into their nest through the gap. When the shutters are down, darkness enters my house and the birds are shut out from their nest. Shutters up, the birds live, shutters down, they perish.

This morning, the shutters were neither up nor down: at half-mast. The cord had been pulled to open the slats and let in some light. Small rectangles of light danced on the bed covers as I sat in my bed writing. I was immediately reminded of a city at nighttime with bright shapes of light among tall black buildings. It felt good to be in this pool of playful light where it was not too bright and not too dark. Here I could write and rest at the same time. Had the shutters been up, the sudden morning brightness would have caused me to squint, had the shutters been down, I would have strained my eyes to see what I was writing. In this in-between light, I felt safe. This is where I needed to be for my writing, I concluded.

The pages were my chicks and, like the blue tits, I was feeding them with plenty of nourishing words. I needed to fatten them up so that one day they would be strong enough to fly out into the world.

Then I remembered that when the shutters are at half mast, the gap is closed, just as it is when the shutters are down. The chicks cannot leave the nest when the gap is closed. I thought about this in connection with my writing and realised that the time will come when I will have to lift the shutters up and let the full light onto the page. Only then can my writing fledge and fly out into the world.

Timing the Growth

I am back in the café of the olympic pool on Kirchberg, Luxembourg after a number of week's absence. It is shortly after midday. My son's school finishes at half past and I must pick him up. I have twenty minutes to write. A few months ago,' I wouldn't have dreamed of slipping into a café and writing an essay like one might slip into a shop to pick up a litre of milk. I wouldn't have considered it enough time. I have learned that I do have the time if I let myself take it. Those twenty minutes could make the difference between a day with, rather than without, writing. I may have some insights. I may just exercise my wrist, or vent some frustrations.

A Seventies song is playing: Say that you love me. Say that you need me. Say that you want me. Say you wanna please me... Oh, I don't want nobody else. All I need is you. You picked me up when I was falling down. And made my life brand new... It is 'Shout' by The Trammps and also the cry of my writer's heart. It's blaring out so loudly I wonder whether it has always been as noisy as this in here.

I told my husband that I wrote at the swimming pool café. He couldn't see that it was conducive. No, it isn't really and yes, it is. It is both loud and silent, depending on what you want to listen to. I can watch the swimmers, divers and the clock: a large face on the far opposite wall. When I write here, the hands go around slower. A second seems like the time it takes a swimmer to complete a length of the 50-metre pool. I can dip into the water with him and write a page in that time. Look, it's not yet half past, another ten minutes and I may have an analogy I could use for my book on the practice of writing.

I saw a poet friend this morning. She talked about her husband's spiritual journey. He began before her. When she started hers, he had already progressed quite far. She delved into his books and things began to move fast for her, too. He got scared she would overtake him. She began to hide her progress, suppressing it so as not to hurt him. She found it hard to keep this up and thought of this analogy: we all set off on our spiritual journeys at different times. We are heading towards the same goal. She sees this goal as God. Her image of God is a large sun, a fireball of light. We are all moving towards the light, she said. If you look at the sun, you will see there are millions upon millions of rays being sent to earth. Some long, some short, some crooked, some straight, some hazy, some clear. She imagines that on every single ray is a person travelling. No two persons are on the same ray; that is how different our paths are. Sometimes they may converge and that will be like a miracle when it does. But the span of time between moments of convergence can be infinite. This is how she sees her and her husband's paths now: very different, sometimes miles apart but always heading towards the same goal - the light.

I have often wished that my husband would embark on a spiritual journey with me. I have yearned for company, guidance, understanding and togetherness. My friend's experience has made it clear that this wish cannot be fulfilled. We journey alone. His path is not my path. It will be his and his alone. It may pull us apart for many years and it may draw us together for ever more.

I need to surrender to this. Let go of the will to make things different. This way I will step into the flow of things and grow as nature intended all along.

Nature will show us the way; yet, all too often, we go against it, digging in with our heels, digging down into darkness rather than letting ourselves be lifted to the light as we are destined to be.

Feeling the Well

How well I feel at the Olympic sports centre. I am back at the pool café with my writing book after weeks of writer's block. I am back up here, on dry ground, looking down at the blue water in which I have just bathed. Half a kilometre I swam. That's 500 metres. Now I drink 500 millilitres of multivitamin juice. I feel like I am pouring the energy I exerted in the pool back in. I have all I need for a successful day: exercise of the body, nutrition and reconnection for the mind through my writing in the atmosphere here. I'm glad I didn't go home. I would have been restless there, fussing about the cooking and the washing and the cleaning lady coming. I would have opened the mailbox and been forced to respond. I would have switched the computer on and spent hours emailing or surfing.

Here, I just write. I have a small plastic table, a piping hot coffee and a vitamin drink. No phone calls, no doorbells, no domestic drills. It's not quiet here; hundreds of children are in the pool and the noise rises up to the café across the domed ceiling. It's one large echo. No individual voices. A mass of noise. It's actually sedating, peaceful; yet full of life and human activity: the occasional splash or bang as a diver jumps from the springboard.

At the adjacent table, there is a young family. They're speaking a Slavic language. Father, mother, toddler daughter. They have bought themselves ice creams. The little girl has sucked off a quarter of it, her nose wrinkling at the coldness in her mouth. She now gives the ice cream to her mother. She doesn't want it anymore. Her mother doesn't really want it, I notice from her expression, but takes it anyway (so it doesn't go to waste, perhaps?). Mum has a round, plump figure. Her husband is thin. He didn't want the extra ice cream from his daughter. The mother eats it. Duty? Or was she hoping from the start that her child would give her some left-overs so she had an excuse to indulge? Is that it? Are we mothers looking for excuses to indulge or are we being obliging and selfless when we eat our child's half-eaten food.

I was in a supermarket when my child was given a piece of sausage by a friendly assistant. He bit a piece off, chewed it, then wanted to spit it out. I was at the cash out. I had no tissue, couldn't throw it discretely on the floor, didn't want to put it in my handbag and felt too embarrassed to ask the cashier. So, what to do? I popped it into my mouth and swallowed.

The echoes drone on, sedating me. I continue writing. It feels like fudge; blocked ideas insisting they are good and sweet. I wonder whether the multivitamin juice is having the opposite effect. Or is it reacting with the coffee making my writer's head cloud over inside like a window attacked by condensation. I know I can't stop here. I will myself to not merely feel the creative well's presence but to dip into it and draw out bucket after bucket and pour it onto the page until my arm aches and I am so sick of myself that I finally manage to get through the murky water and out into the clear creative pool.

Plucking Eyebrows

My sister could turn the tide of my mood with little effort. I was so mad once that she again hadn't tidied her part of our tiny bedroom that I plucked my eyebrows. I attacked each hair with the tweezers as if I were pulling out one of her teeth. I felt triumphant: plucking my eyebrows had been something I had wanted to do for months, but hadn't found the courage to face the pain to do so.

Today, decades later, I find myself raging inside like the day I plucked my eyebrows. I feel like shouting at everyone to get out of my house and my life. Since 8 am, workmen have been in here clanking, hammering, slamming and shouting. The kids have been running, screaming, jumping and arguing. It is now 6 p.m. and I have had it up to my eyebrows. It's time to pluck them out.

I will announce a strike tomorrow. The boys will be allowed to do as they please all day. I shall do as I please all day. I shall not demand anything from them. I will not nag or tick them off. There will be no rules until 6 p.m. They can vegetate, procrastinate, agitate, litigate, and anything else they innovate. I will do the same. I will not prepare breakfast, lunch or tea. I will not tell them to get dressed, brush their teeth, wash their hands or be kind to their brother. I will not tell them to switch the television on or off, or stop playing on the Nintendo.

I am throwing in the towel - for now - and will let disarray pour in like the rainwater into the brook behind the house. It is so full, it is bursting out of its bed, gushing over stones, rocks, spilling into my garden, sweeping across the lawn. I know that some worms will drown, perhaps the moles, too, and slugs galore could be whipped off the lettuce heads and sent running into the woods.

The vegetable patch and I will be triumphant.

Sacre Coeur

Walking down the street at 49, the city is Paris, springtime. A wind picks up the winter dust around my feet and blows cherry blossom at me. I look down at my shoes; a petal has landed on the tip of my black trainers and sits stubbornly, accusingly. 'Have you forgotten?' I quicken my pace and stamp my feet; I'm in a rush to get to the Sacre Coeur for a midday rendez-vous with Susan.

The petal is still on my shoe when I climb onto the snorting metro and squeeze through elbows, bags and backs to a free space. As I stand there, holding onto the cold metal pole, the petal slips to the floor - a speck of softness in a forest of stiff human legs. Without thinking, I reach down, gather it into my palm and gently enclose it, making sure I leave a little pocket of air for it to breathe.

Cherry blossom? No, I haven't forgotten. The English cul-de-sac was lined with cherry trees that blossomed every April. Everything behind the trees was seen as if through a pair of pink-tainted glasses. The air was so full of the brightness of the blossoms that it wiped every kind of sky clear of any grey. The trees functioned as wings, curtain and backdrop to our childhood play: bicycle races, obstacle courses, tree climbing, street chalking and picnics. We would play for hours and hours, stopping only when our mothers called us inside. We were happy-go-lucky children in our pink-coloured realm, protected from life backstage, full of rickety steps and trap doors.

Those trees witnessed everything including the first flirts and fights; they also enhanced the red on our cheeks when you unexpectedly plonked a kiss on my twelve-year-old lips and your sister slapped you for it.

It was also under the cherry trees, ten years later, not in England, but in Washington DC that you proposed and I told you I did not love you enough to give up my job, move and become your wife.

My dear Peter, I am at the Sacre Coeur and have just met Susan. I was surprised when she called to say she was in Paris and wanted to meet up - we have had little contact over the years. She never did like the fact that you loved me.

She was standing waiting when I arrived. She grabbed me, pulled me to her and kissed me on my lips. I was not ready for it - are we ever ready for anything in life? I often think I am but then I stumble and fall over the same step and realise I am stuck in a never-ending rehearsal.

Then came the slap... strong and sharp; a swift sword jabbing the accompanying words deep into my heart as if she wanted to kill me with them. She thrust your letter into my arms and left me standing there, staring at the Sacre Coeur. She always was the most dramatic girl I ever knew.

I have always loved you Peter. You are part of my history, my childhood. I am sorry I did not marry you all those years ago, and that you found no other solution than to end your life. This cherry blossom in my hand is all that is left. I shall take it into the Sacre Coeur now.

Perhaps my words will find their way to you, wherever you are, and bring peace.

This is my prayer.

Travelling to the Yoke

I have settled for the cold metal chair on platform 3AB to wait for the Luxembourg to Brussels Intercity via Namur. A loudspeaker announces in French, German and Luxembourgish that the train will be ten to fifteen minutes late and so I have time to write. How perfect. Everything has its place; its time.

I have a spring in my step; it is my spirit rejoicing and dancing. My husband brought me to the station. He said goodbye to me and I skipped away and out of sight. I am aglow about taking myself on this trip to the capital city of Belgium, alone. I am off on an adventure: a voyage of uncovery, rather than discovery, I decide.

As I write that down, I suddenly realise the significance of it. Brussels was where my husband and I met; I am visiting the source of our original love. When my husband asked at breakfast what I was going to do there, I simply replied that I would see where the trip took me and continued to dig the soft orange centre out of my egg with a piece of bread. The bread was cut into what the British often call soldiers - thin strips that can be dipped into the egg and come out with a coating of runny yoke. I am like the bread soldier, our relationship is the egg. At the centre of the relationship is the yoke - an orange sun reflected in a white ocean. I am trying to find that yoke and dip into it again.

The terracotta-coloured chair in the EC train compartment to Brussels-Midi feels like a feathered cushion to my backside and I let myself sink into it. The journey will last three hours. I should be in the middle of Brussels by midday! This fact makes me hopeful that the tracks will carry me straight and true through the hilly Ardennes to the heart of European Unification and my marriage.

*

We met in 1988 at a business conference held at the Holiday-Inn hotel in close vicinity to Brussels airport. At that time, I was managing electronic dictionaries for a machine translation system at a UK-based company and he was managing documents for the same machine-translation system at a Germany-based company. Brussels was not quite midway, but definitely neutral ground and was the place our two lives were brought together. This meeting was planned by destiny, of that I am sure. We were prepared (pre-paired, I would say) three years previously in Saarbrücken, Germany where I spent a year working on a project as part of my university degree course with Manchester University and where he worked for a time on that same project as a way to gain translation experience for his degree course with Saarbrücken University.

Some delegates gathered in the hotel bar before the start of the conference. He ended up sitting next to me, turned to look at me and announced: "Haven't we met somewhere before?"

He remembered and by doing so, reminded me that I had met him before. This simple act of remembrance lifted the catch that released the ball that triggered the relationship. Is that the mechanics of life? We remember and remind and then the path lays itself out before us?

*

A week ago, I unpacked the slides and projector from their box where they had remained unwanted for two house moves. I lay tray after tray of slides onto the projector arm and that arm lead us down many dusty paths: more than a decade of togetherness. Some of the dust on those paths was grey, some multi-coloured, and some golden. We let some dust settle on us as slide after slide was slipped into the light by the mechanical arm of the projector. Golden dust landed on us that evening during the slide show. Not all of it has been blown off, I note now.

The day is cloudless, yet hazy. The horizon looks like a glass where milk once was. All that is left is the white trace for the washer up to see and deal with. I am the washer up in our marriage. I know this the moment I write it, not before. The milky weather this morning speaks optimistically of a clear afternoon - as long as the sunrays reach far enough to wipe the milky remains off the new morning sky. I wonder what the Ardennes will have to say about it. They may send down a few clouds for the sun to deal with. The wind too will play its part. It may blow more clouds in the sun's path, or it may blow them westward to await sunset. The sun will decide the outcome of the day; it will determine whether the wisps of cloud will turn into a thick blanket cover or be evaporated into a translucent blue.

When I arrived home yesterday from a day out of the house, my husband greeted me with a romantic idea: let's take the bikes and a bottle of wine and ride out into the hills to watch the sunset. I jumped with joy at his suggestion. He said to give him half an hour to finish his job (he was tiling the front-door step) and then we'll go. I made us both a cup of tea and waited. One and three-quarter hours later, we set off. He had underestimated the time he needed for the tiling job. 'Each tile has to be measured and hand cut before it can be fixed into place,' he later lamented. 'It is a long and tricky job and the amount of time needed cannot be predicted.' I thought about the way he approached our relationship and could understand why we ended up racing on the bikes to catch a glimpse of the sunset before it was gobbled up by the wooded hills of the valley in which we lived. He approaches the relationship as a tiler tiling the front door step. He cuts and trims and polishes the tiles on the outside and spends large amounts of time, patience and energy getting them into perfect place. He takes great pride in his work and precision, his calculations, predictions and organisation. Is he so busy on the exterior, getting it all to fit, that he neglects the interior?

The train has reached the hills. The sky is heavy with contemplative cloud: shall we rain now or later? Rain does not come, but I know the clouds are full-to-bursting. Are the clouds enjoying the tension of the atmosphere? Anticipation and fear hang over the hilltops and turn the spring morning into a menacing brew which makes me ponder what it must feel like in the transitional period between life and death. Are we in that in-between moment now in our relationship?

There are evergreens in the valleys. The deciduous trees are late in receiving their leaves here in this higher region. The only sign of spring is the white-speckled hawthorn blossoms flashing furiously as the train speeds past.

I feel safe inside the empty train compartment. I do not have to expose myself to the atmospheric tension outside. I can look at it and consider its potential for ruining my day, but I can stay inside where it is dry and quiet. That is my position in the marriage right now; safe inside where I know who I am and am sure of the path I am travelling on. From the inside I can see the outside - the exterior forces on our relationship. I can pull my observations into the dry inside and use them to understand, to obtain greater knowledge and thus greater growth. The sun touches my shoulder as I write those words – I consider it a compassionate pat of encouragement.

The train has travelled through the highest peaks of the Ardennes out into the foothills and the sky is clearing. Houses appear and with them more variation in the vegetation and more diverse colours. We are back with the human touch and I appreciate the reds, purples, oranges and blacks – in cars, doors, gardens. Forsythia splashes yellow here and there like spilled paint. That looks too untidy, my husband would say and salivate at the thought of cutting the branches back; creating order out of chaos.

*

I wonder whether his condemnation of nature's untidy way of announcing spring has to do with being German, in the same way, perhaps that order and precision had prevailed over an untimely sunset. Keep order and precision in nature and in mind. Never let the heart decide. Intuition and instinct are dangerous paths to follow. Are these his maxims? Where do they come from? Could they come from a deep mistrust passed on through the collective German unconscious? If this is so, maybe I do understand our relationship and the path we are on together.

German blood runs through us both. Born of an English father and German mother, my German-ness has been diluted. Perhaps that is why I find it easier to take an intuitive approach in life, moving from country to country, from job to job, from path to path by listening to my heart. My husband was born of German parents. Parents, who, like my mother's parents, believed Hitler, initially. He spoke to their hearts and got them to follow and have faith in his plan for a brighter future. The horror when they realised the grotesqueness of his *Kampf*. They had been tempted by the devil himself and did not see him until it was too late - until the whole world knew. Oh the shame, the guilt. How could they ever know their true nature again?

My husband's generation; children born in the twenty years after the war may have wriggled free of the guilt, but trust in human nature is still lacking. *Never again will I follow my heart and lay trust in another's hands*, I hear his unconscious voice say. *My parents did so and look what happened. They allowed themselves to be tempted by the devil. I will always be cautious and untrusting of fellow humans. Even when my heart tells me it is the right way; I will not follow that route. I will plan and cut and shape and puzzle until I have made a way for myself that fits. I will not believe my heart. The way of the heart may be the wrong way: the way of destruction and evil, not of good.*

Is this what people who lived through the Hitler period have passed on to their children? Are these the thoughts necessary to guard themselves from manipulation a second time? If so, I can understand the power of such a consciousness. My husband and all of his generation carry a heavy weight with them on their road through life.

*

Brussels is a new city for me. When I met my husband there thirteen years ago, I never got further than the conference room of the Holiday Inn hotel. Even so, I didn't want to find out about the city before I went. I didn't want to read the guide and form an opinion or have any expectations. I wanted to go and see and watch and listen to what the city had to say to me. I suppose I am protesting against admiring a town, a building, a square or park just because the guide has told me to. I shun preconceived ideas. I like to approach a new place as a clear slate and fill it with experience. In the past, I misinterpreted this desire for pure, unadulterated experience as the wrong way to approach anything new. I told myself that I was just too lazy to read up about the place.

Now I realise that I was simply not aware. Through writing I become aware and learn to trust my way of learning and growing. Each time clarity comes, I am surprised by its richness. I know little about the great thinkers and philosophers, but when I come across thoughts and theories from Freud, Jung, Homer, Plato, I find I do know - I know because I can understand. I understand, not because I have access to knowledge acquired from school, university or books, but because it slots in. It slots in because it fits in with the way I think and experience. Learning and becoming knowledgeable becomes simple when it is not forced but experienced. It is innocent knowledge. It is truth.

Each time I look out of the window, more and more blue is revealed to me. The sky is undressing and the clouds have been cast to the wind to float like negligees in an azure ocean. Cows are lying down in the fields - a sign that the threat of rain has not yet passed. The silver birch are shining in the sun and the leaves are so new that they look artificial, as if someone has glued them on as decoration.

The train moves briskly on and enters the city. Here the landscape has been tamed into gardens, car parks and communal areas with perimeter fences. They belong to houses, blocks of flats, companies. Graffiti greets new arrivals in the station entrance - an encoded message known only by the owner of the spray can. Pigeons flap and displace themselves a lazy metre. We have arrived in Brussels-Nord, or Brussel-Noord as the next sign announces. The train is running behind schedule. I don't mind.

I see a brief flash of blue sky and tongue of white cloud before the train plunges into darkness. A tunnel. All I see now is the regular flashing of brightness as the tunnel lights whiz past the window. I feel disorientated here below the city, unable to latch onto a light or a point of orientation. I would much rather travel over the surface. It's easier to see your way. Down here there is only darkness. All man-made: concrete, suburban civilisation. Its drabness deadens me.

Where most of human life is, is where I feel least human and least alive. In the hills I know where I am. In the concrete tunnel, I cannot know when it will end and bring me to my destination.

Submersing myself in a city full of people, concrete and commercialism, stifles me; makes me want to spit this part of humanness out. I feel like an exotic bird out of place and uncomfortable as if in a zoo, owned by the city.

Brussel-Sud, Brussel-Zuid, signs loom up and shock me. We have travelled under the city from north to south. I presume the tunnel took us along the perimeter and the train will next head for the centre, Brussels-Midi. The centre is where I have chosen to be: in the middle of it all. I stay in my seat holding on to its warmness and comfort, looking out of the window wondering when the train is going to jerk into motion again. A conductor and assistant come into my compartment. 'The train ends here,' they announce, 'You have to get off!' I am confused. 'You mean it's not going on to the central station, Brussels-Midi?' I ask with some urgency. They smile. 'This is Midi, Madame,' they say in unison. 'But it says Sud,' I protest. 'Sud is the same as Midi, Madame,' they say. I am embarrassed and as I climb off the train, I remember the French phrase 'midi de la France' from school meaning the South of France and that I had often been mis-lead by it back then.

I wander out of the station and onto the main road. I look at the street map I have with me but can't find the street names. I ask a lady standing at a tram stop to point me in the direction of the Grande Place, the central square in Brussels. She obliges and I set off, following the train tracks as she instructed me to do. The large avenue is empty. Midday, I think to myself, the people will be having lunch. I am self-conscious walking down the large avenue alone, in a strange city. I quicken my pace and add dark glasses to my face. The route into the city from the station is taking me through an Arab quarter and as I move along the road towards the centre, I notice more and more groups of Arab men on the streets, chatting, sitting in cafes, standing at street corners. I wonder if it is a wise choice to walk into the city centre and try to remember what the lady at the tram stop had said. She had tried to explain to me why she wasn't walking into the city, but taking the tram. I hadn't taken the trouble to listen carefully, or understand. Now I wonder, had she said something about it being dangerous?

My eyes search around for something familiar. I spot two young girls on the opposite side of the avenue - on the other side of

266

the tramline. They are wearing pedal pushers and have modern haircuts - students perhaps. I cross over and follow them until they take a right turn and disappear into a building. I continue. An empty square is all that greets me at the end of the avenue. I was expecting to be in the middle of a busy shopping street. I glance around at the shops. All closed. Lunch?

I look up and see the Mercedes star emblem on a high-rise I'd seen from the train near to Gare du Nord. I didn't want to end up there and miss the centre! I move diagonally across the square, continuing straight on and then taking a right. The first thing I see is a souvenir shop. I never thought I would welcome that sight. The shop is selling Belgian lace, the peeing fountain boy, European Institution souvenirs, cups with 'I love Brussels' printed on them, little models of Belgian houses, waffles, seafood - anything and everything that could be sold under the name of 'souvenir' - to remember.

*

When I lived in Germany on a sabbatical year after finishing 'A' level and before starting university - I went on trips and collected little glasses from the German towns and cities I visited. I have no idea where they are now. Probably in a junk shop, in the bin or lost between one of the many house moves I have made since. In my collection I had Heidelberg, Regensburg, Ulm, München, Berlin, Lübeck and Köln. They cost DM 3,-. That was the price of the nutritious sandwich I often forfeited to purchase it. A souvenir, pah! The best souvenirs I could have are memories and they are forever in my mind and often land on the page as I write - quite by chance - reminding me of my experiences and who I am.

*

My wanderings lead me to the tourist information centre and a shelf full of brochures. One in particular stands out from the rest. It announces an exhibition of German Expressionists at the Musée d'Ixelles. The collection of paintings has been called 'Die Brücke' (The Bridge). I tell the man behind the counter that I would like to go there and could he advise me. He gives me instructions and I set off enthusiastically. I must have headed in the wrong direction because I end up on Place des Herbes and not Rue de la Bourse as he said I would. I sit down at the fountain in the middle of Place des Herbes, let droplets of water spray on my back as I scrutinise the street map once more. It is hopeless. I am disorientated and don't feel like working it out.

I decide to forget the exhibition and set off the way I had come, hoping to get back to the Grande Place, the central square, where I would stay, circling it, so that I would not get lost. I retrace my steps and arrive back at the Grande Place with ease. I look across to the side I had originally entered by, just to reassure myself that I will find my way back to the Brussels-Midi station when it is time to leave at around 5.

I walk on through the back streets around the Grande Place. One restaurant after another entices people to come and enjoy seafood specialities at their heated street tables. When I emerge from the labyrinth of back streets and restaurants, I find myself in Rue de la Bourse. Oh, I think, maybe I will go to the art exhibition after all. I continue up the street and it leads me to the Bourse building. Opposite is a Metro sign, just as the man at the tourist information centre said there would be. It looks like the underground, he had said, but it is actually a tram stop. I climb down the steps and ask for a return ticket to Place E. Flagey on the No. 81 tram. He gives me two tickets and tells me to descend another flight of steps to the tram platform. There is only one platform at the bottom of the steps. I was expecting two - one in each direction. Before I have time to do anything about the second thoughts I am having, the tram arrives. I climb on and sit next to a window. After a couple of underground stops, the tram rises up to the noisy streets. I didn't have a chance to ask the driver when I got on the tram whether it was going to Place E. Flagey and I don't want to give up my seat next to the window. The tram is full. The man sitting opposite me looks respectable so I ask him whether he knows Place E. Flagey. He doesn't. But he says that the stations are marked and I am sure not to miss it. It's beyond Brussels-Midi he says and then gets off himself in Brussels-Midi. Good, I think, if I am on the wrong tram and don't find the Musée d'Ixelles, at least I will be able to get back to the station for my return journey.

A black man comes to sit opposite me. I nudge him

accidentally with my leg when the tram shakes into motion again. 'Excusez-moi' I say and he nods. I'll ask him, I think. He has to extract earphones from his ears. I had failed to see he was listening to music on his Walkman. I wouldn't have disturbed him if I had known that. He smiles. 'Je vais montrer,' he announces. I'll show you. Oh dear, I thought. Have I made a mistake? I don't know if I want him to show me! He smiles again when I catch his eye. Is it a coy or sly smile? I feel myself mistrusting this black man. Maybe he will abduct me and rape me. Maybe he will tell me where to get off and it won't be Place E. Flagey but somewhere near his home and he'll grab me and take me there and … My imagination runs wild and I look around nervously for orientation. I must take some responsibility. I must have an idea where I am. The tram stops at a square. The name of the stop is 'Bethlehem'. The train moves on. The black man stirs. Is this Place E. Flagey? He looks at me and holds up a hand, pink palm facing me and fingers spread. 'Encore 5 arrêtes,' he says. Another five stops. I begin to calm down. How sweet, I reflect, he has noticed my anxiety and has taken the trouble to calculate the number of stops. I decide that I can trust him and look around me, more relaxed.

The next stop I take any notice of is called 'Wilhelm Tell'. How appropriate a name for this trip, I muse. Next comes 'La Maison Blanche' - the White House. It was, in fact, the name of a café on the corner next to the stop and it was far from white or grand. How funny! Here I am on my way to the German expressionists going through Schiller's Wilhelm Tell which I studied as part of my A-Level German course at school, past the White House, which I visited when going out with an American History student, on to 'The Bridge' (die Brücke).

Am I going on a more significant journey than I thought? I ask myself. I did not plan to take the tram. In fact, I had resigned and was prepared to keep on circling the Grande Place until it was time to return to Luxembourg. Now the day has taken me on its journey. It is as if it has seized me.

Place E. Flagey arrives. There is no mistaking it. And it was indeed 5 stops further as the black man had said. He is already standing at the door, chatting to a woman - obviously a friend. I say goodbye and thank you as I descend the steep tram steps. I look around for signs to the museum. There are none. I turn around and am suddenly face to face with the black man again. Don't you know where you are going? he asks. I shake my head and show him the brochure. He says to ask a taxi driver and points to a taxi stand further down the street.

The taxi driver is friendly and helpful. His instructions get me up a hill and take me left. There is still no sign of the museum. I land in a residential area and am convinced I have gone wrong. I look at the road name: 'Sans Souci' (carefree). This can't be right with a name like that, I think and look for a way back to the main road. I take a right down a road called 'Viaduc' and on reaching the end, finally spot a sign for the museum. It is pointing in the direction I have just come. Surely I can't have walked right passed it? I turn back. Another sign takes me left, another sign left again. It feels like I am going around in circles and wonder for the third time whether it is all worth my while. Just as I am beginning to give up, I see the museum building up ahead.

I have arrived. Am I really going back to my roots, my German heritage, and the source of my marriage? Back to my ancestors and links to my artist sister whose work is often praised for the Germanic expressionist influence? Is this what my journey today is all about? Making the circle round, becoming whole? - not just myself, but also my marriage and our shared unconscious.

I walk through the museum like one might walk reverently through a church to the altar. It has a strange familiarity about it. It is as if I know the paintings before having seen them. Nolte and co. are there. I recognise them from my sister's art. I see their expressions in her expressions. People, scenes, nature.

Then I come to a picture by Mueller called 'Deux Jeunes Filles dans un Bois.' (two young girls in a wood). The piece of work looks like one of the scribbled sketches my five-year-old son makes. On closer examination, I realise what makes it so special: the girls have become part of the trees and the wood itself. From a distance, they are hardly discernible. Yet, close up, you can see they are the roots and the trunks and the leaves and the branches. They symbolise life and wisdom, nature and freedom.

Everything begins to make sense. I was born to German-English parents, brought up in British culture and language. I married a German and bring up dual-nationality, bilingual children in Luxembourg - a neutral country- neither English nor German.

Now I am in Brussels, the heart of Europe, home of the European Institutions and where I met my partner, husband, and father of my children. Here I am seized by the day and taken to the German Expressionists exhibition: The Bridge. A souvenir. A bridge to, and reminder of the past?

On the train I wrote about my German heritage, about the collective guilt, about judging and mistrust. On the tram, I myself judged and mistrusted my guide - the black man who was telling me the way. Twice I mistrusted my journey and myself. Now I am here and I feel I have travelled full circle and into the yoke. I am looking at the expressions of Germans and seeing my family and myself in them. I am a stranger, a foreigner in Brussels and yet I have found where I belong. Here I feel I truly have come to 'die Brücke' - the bridge. This bridge is like an arc, the other half of the circle, the part that makes it round, whole. This is what my journey is about and my writing. I feel sure of it now.

I buy a catalogue - a souvenir to remind me of the day. I ask the man in the shop how to get back to Place E. Flagey - the direct route. He tells me to go out of the museum, turn left and then descend: 'toujours descendre, toujours descendre' and you'll get there. I thank him and know he is absolutely right. It is an easy descent from here.

I go to collect my rucksack from the cloakroom. That's a heavy load you are carrying, the girl remarks as she heaves it over the counter. Yes, I reflect, but I can carry it with more ease after my journey today.

Berlinese Impressions

The aircraft flew along a cloud-filled corridor in the sky above East Berlin. Suddenly the plane dipped as if it had stumbled over a step and my stomach lurched. As the plane broke through the clouds and the city of East Berlin was revealed below, the Television Tower[22] loomed so large I imagined I could have touched it if I had been able to open the window and reach out. From my vantage point, the Berlin Wall was a mere strip of white, the watch towers in so-called 'no-man's land', regular white squares and the thousands of spotlights, tiny dots.

The approach to Tegel airport carried us over the rooftops of East Berlin, over the wall, over the rooftops of West Berlin and on to land on the runway. I imagined birds, insects and all other of nature's flying creatures making a similar route every day, unaware of the significance of the white strip, squares and dots.

Waiting for my luggage at the conveyor belt, I couldn't help but be audience to a woman announcing to everyone around her how primitive Berlin was. She was indignant that the taxi driver had refused to wait for her at the exit whilst she collected her baggage – and that she would now have to stand in line for a taxi like everyone else. She reminded me of a New Yorker who climbed into the Greyhound bus before we had time to get off, or the bus had been prepared for the next journey and complained that it was unbearably stuffy, full and hot. She was right of course: the bus had just taken over 40 passengers from the east to the west coast of America over a grueling three nights and two days nonstop.

Berlin primitive? By no means!

My taxi driver negotiated his way through Berlin's morning traffic with alarming speed, showing off his driving skills around the

---

[22] Fernsehturm in former East Berlin. It had monument status in the German Democratic Republic and this status was perpetuated after German reunification.

so-called Großer Stern[23], a large roundabout encircling the Victory Column[24] (where he said that the same rules applied as for British roundabouts, but that he didn't agree with them), and I arrived at my hotel, the Hotel Savoy, with pearls of perspiration forming on my brow as if I had run across the near-by Ernst-Reuter Platz and been sprayed upon by its 41 fountains .

Summer seemed to have arrived in Berlin. For the first time, I was struck by the city's lushness and the many shades of green. I could hear birdsong everywhere – even in streets a stone's throw from the main traffic routes through the heart of the city.

The atmosphere was like that of a Parisian boulevard in the height of the summer season: street cafés, street artists, street markets, tourists.

The Berliners seemed to strut along the streets, proud to be Berliners even if their claim to being a Berliner was only by virtue of living and working there for many years. Rather a Berliner, though, than the other category – the so-called Wessi – people from the rest of West Germany; they were frowned upon and had become a favourite subject in jokes and comedy shows.

In the Jazz bar, 'Go In' in Bleibtreu Strasse, a young singer continued unabashed to sing her song about the Wessi despite the place being full of them and their agitation becoming tangible. In the Quartier Latin, the three comedians, Die drei Tornados joked that every Wessi claimed to know you, even if it was a friend of a friend of a friend met whilst on holiday in Greece twenty years ago – just so that they could come and visit! What a horror it was for a Berliner when a Wessi came to visit. All the Wessi wanted to do was walk through the run-down and dangerous streets of Kreuzberg, snoop around the famous courtyards[25] of the historic Kreuzberg houses, climb onto the purpose-built platforms to peer over the wall at East Berlin, take thousands of photos of this strange

---

[23] Literally, Large Star - a central intersection from which fives avenues stretch out like points of a star in different directions.
[24] Siegessäule
[25] So-called Hinterhöfe

phenomenon, including the guards as they kept an eye on them through binoculars. Then they had to drink plenty of Berliner Weisse at Jo's on the Ku' Damm and stay up for the nightlife in the city that never sleeps.

Night life – it lived up to its name. Life in bars began at 10.30 p.m. and continued past the normal closing time of bars in the rest of West Germany.

Jazz bars, Blues & Rock Kneipen[26], Irish pubs, French cafès...the list of watering houses was endless as was the imagination that went into making them authentic and unique. In one place, all the original decor remained unchanged from when it used to be a brothel[27]: red, green and gold carpet covered floor, ceiling and bar. Velvet curtains hung from archways and alcoves along with plenty of kitsch, plastic flowers and lamps.

At the Café Hardenberg, half way between Ernst-Reuter Platz and the main station Bahnhof Zoo, the young trendies and students would drink a Patz or two and eat broccoli baked with ham and cheese. A joke did the rounds: how do find out which side of the wall is West Berlin and which is East Berlin? You simply place a banana on top of the wall and leave it there for a few days. The side that is bitten is East.

Walking down Fasanen Strasse on the last evening in downtown Berlin with a Wessi friend, I literally stumbled upon (excuse the pun) the Literary Café[28] – a café housed in a belle époque villa with conservatory and garden.

I sat under a large oak tree with a Patz and wrote down my impressions of West Berlin on this warm spring day in May 1989.

Who would have imagined that in just a few months, the Berlin Wall would come tumbling down, the Ossi[29] would arrive and Berliners would be referred to as Wessi.

---

[26] Kneipe is German for pub or bar.

[27] Kumpelnest 3000

[28] Literary Café is a translation. The original name is Literaturhaus.

[29] Ossi is the term that was used to refer to those who came from former East Germany, the >German Democratic Republic, DDR

Fricassée Argenteuil

Fricassée Argenteuil, she reads, is a vegetable dish that takes its name from Argenteuil near Paris, famous for asparagus. She closes the cookery book and glances at the asparagus lying in their paper wrapping on the draining board. All thirty point accusingly at her kitchen tiles that still show traces of her last culinary disaster. The brown speckles on the once white tiles are from marmalade that never reached the preserve jars and are a permanent reminder of her last attempt at cooking something in front of Olivier, her French boyfriend. Not that she could blame that catastrophe on him. She was learning the hard way that she was better at reading computer programs than recipes. Olivier still joked about the way the pressure cooker spewed its contents across the tiles like spray-can graffiti and when he did, a sense of failure returned and she no longer believed she was worthy of being his girlfriend. After all, he was raised on French gourmet meals prepared by his mother whose family fortune came from restaurants with Michelin stars.

She sighs again and again as she collects the necessary utensils and ingredients for her work. Most are poor-me sighs, a few are sighs of frustration and the rest are sighs of anger at her current predicament. It all started last Friday, the day of her promotion to head programmer in the computer company she worked for in Brighton, UK. She had invited her close colleagues, including Olivier, to some celebratory champagne and ended up drinking it all herself. The subject of good food and wine had come up because her colleagues were pleased to have an expert in their midst (Olivier, of course) and, feeling radiant and completely under the influence of alcohol, she had impulsively invited them all to ' a dinner to remember' at her place. The words had just slipped out and now she would have to live up to them.

'What shall I cook for you, then?' she had asked, not really expecting anyone to reply. Olivier had jumped up straight away and exclaimed: Fricassée Argenteuil' and promptly dropped a French cookbook into her lap as if he'd been waiting for that moment all his life.

That was last Friday – an altogether fuzzy day due to all the champagne – and now it was Saturday and she was alone in her kitchen with the task of mastering 'Fricassée Argenteuil' – her boyfriend's favourite childhood dish. During her two-year relationship with him, Olivier had always made her feel that she more than lived up to his expectations. Now she was not so sure. His request for this dish had unnerved her. Did he expect her to be as good a cook as his mother?

She opens the cookbook at the right page (Olivier has earmarked it for her) and a sheet of paper flashes his beautiful handwriting at her as it flies out like a single-winged bird and lands next to the cooker. It is an English translation of the recipe. She seizes it, twists it and jets it into the bin. Was he teasing her again? He knows perfectly well that her French was as good as his English, so why the translation? Was he making sure that if the dish went wrong, she wouldn't be able to place the blame on the French?

She slams the metal colander down on the counter: 'I shall make this dish – and fantastically – if it's the last thing I do,' she resolves.

Clean the asparagus, the recipe dictates. She runs the cold tap and pushes the asparagus into the sink like lemmings over a cliff edge. The water splashes her face and the spears make a sound on the bottom like distant drums. She takes out one at a time, rubs it from tip to end and back up again and places it back into the colander, pleased that she rejected Olivier's offer of help: he would have loved how she handled the asparagus, attaching sexual inuendo to her every move.

When all the asparagus is finally clean and back in the colander, she heaves a sigh of relief. All thirty tips peer at her and she wonders what her work colleagues would have said about that, too. They had joked about the phallic nature of the food all last week, laughing more than they had laughed about anything in a long time. She didn't think it was at all funny.

She takes the sharpest knife she owns from the knife block, as she recalls one of the numerous pieces of advice Olivier had given her over the week. Each helpful hint had been offered in a half-serious, half-jovial manner so that she couldn't establish whether he was teasing or had genuinely wanted to be helpful. By Friday, she had not only been confused, but also exasperated from all the information she had received. Yet it was impossible to get

276

angry with him because, when she did, his French lips pursed in such an irresistible way that she just wanted to feast on him. As far as she was concerned, he was the only gourmet meal she needed.

It seemed that Fricassée Argenteuil' was more important to him, and, if she wanted to have him, she would have to master it.

Cut off the woody ends and discard. She lines the asparagus up ten at a time, slices through them and throws those so-called woody ends into the kitchen compost bin. Then she realigns what is left and cuts, realigns and cuts, realigns and cuts, enjoying how the knife slices through them with ease and grace. Before she realises what she is doing, the damage has been done and is irreversible: the asparagus have been made into a hundred rods of stubs no longer than her thumb nail. Even the tips don't meet the required length of 2.5 cm for the dish. Olivier would surely notice if she included them and his gourmet eye would certainly not approve, even though they were supposed to be the best part. Oh well, she thinks, looks at them lovingly and then throws them into the bin. *If only Olivier could have seen her professional knife strokes!*

The only bits that would be long enough are the woody ends that are still lying amongst the potato peelings in the compost bin. She picks them out, rinses them off and performs a tenderness test with the tip of her knife. They pass. She then arranges them prettily in the casserole.

She is now feeling quite creative and can suddenly understand how Olivier must feel every day of his life. He was so creative that he could rustle up a three-star menu from left-overs in the fridge. She preferred to organise and manage and, up to now, had thought that he liked the fact that she had those contrasting qualities. He had called them 'complémentaire'. Or was it 'contradictoire'? She's no longer sure.

To console herself, she opens the bottle of wine Olivier had given to her and pours herself a full glass. The twenty-year old Grand Premier Cru Classé from his grandmother's wine cellar that was supposed to 'breathe' before the meal so that it would be at its best once they ate, tastes alright now as far as she can tell and she gulps it down. It is then that she remembers that she was supposed to have bought a selection of extra wine and cheese (Olivier had written a detailed list) from the local wine shop and delicatessen. No doubt the guests will bring some as host presents, she thinks and pours herself another glass.

She is in full swing, submerged in the smells and sounds around the hob, enjoying the wine: cooking can be pleasurable, she thinks and resolves to do it more often. Not for him – but for herself.

That is the main problem in their relationship, she reflects. She fell in love and started doing things to please him: French lessons, visits to Paris, museums, holidays in Brittany, French wine tasting. It had been thrilling, romantic, delicious. But where was the relationship going? How compliant would she let herself become? Was she hoping he would propose? She wishes that she'd booked a table at a popular fish and chip restaurant on Brighton Pier instead.

The bottle is nearly empty by the time she gets to the trickiest part of the recipe – the thickening of the sauce.

Stir rapidly to prevent lumps from forming, she reads.

Her sauce had lumps even before she started stirring and are now multiplying more rapidly than cancer cells. A wave of indignation comes over her. She no longer cares what the meal will be like and encourages larger lumps to form by adding spoonfuls of flour to the boiling liquid. It's child's play. Finally, she steps back to admire her creation: Fricassée à la Lump, she exclaims in exaltation and thinks that this will certainly be a dinner to remember.

The doorbell rings and she opens it with the grace and composure of one who has everything under control. Only five of her colleagues greet her. The sixth, the others explain, is fetching something and will be along shortly. Olivier, they announce, will be arriving late because he had to fly to Paris for some urgent business. The sixth finally arrives lugging a hold-all that he explains is an overnight bag in case he gets too drunk. Seeing as no-one has brought any wine, she doubts whether he will get even slightly tipsy on Perrier alone.

Olivier still hasn't arrived by nine-thirty. Her guests have been politely sipping Perrier and nibbling bread sticks in anticipation of the subsequent wine and meal, when she finally asks them to sit at the table. She is about to serve the first spoon when the doorbell rings. She runs to open it hopeful that it might be Olivier. It's not. It's a taxi driver who says he's been sent by Olivier to get her and take her to him. It's an emergency, he says.

She has no other choice but to go. The taxi driver takes her to a building and ushers her through the door. Inside, Olivier is sitting at a table set for two behind candles and a bottle of wine.

I'm sorry I gave you a fright, he says, but I had every good reason.

She sits down and her blood prickles as it journeys back up her body from her feet. Olivier gives her a card that looks like a menu, but is actually a mock computer program:

Tonight's Special

If NO asparagus
THEN fish and chips
AND mushy peas
ELSE
GO TO box under chair

She leans over her seat and dips her hand into the darkness. Her fingers bump into a velvet box which she lifts onto the table and opens.

'I will,' she says.

Man's Unsexy Wife

Once upon a time in the days of great knowledge and technological advancement, a man was attacked by the modern and fashionable disease called *victimitis*. It didn't hurt. There were no spots or rashes or vomiting or coughing. In fact, he didn't even realise he had caught the disease because he looked and felt no different than before.

No wonder, for *victimitis* was a very clever disease. It got into peoples' heads and tampered with their view of things, making them believe that their suffering had nothing to do with them; it was others and the world around them that was making them feel this way.

One day, the man who had caught *victimitis* without realising it, complained to his wife that he had no sex life anymore. Being a sufferer of the disease, he could only see what was wrong with her and how she was not meeting his sexual needs. 'It is all your fault,' he said, 'you are always too tired, too disinterested or too preoccupied with other things in your life to pay attention to my sexual needs!'

His wife, a woman who had once herself been a sufferer of *victimitis*, recognised the symptoms and refused to take the blame. 'The last time we had sex was 5 days ago,' she reminded him, 'hardly an indication that we have 'no sex life anymore!'".

Knowing that exaggeration and over-generalisation were symptoms of *victimitis,* she was immediately alarmed. The wife also knew that, in face of any problem or criticism, she must ask herself what she needed to realise about the situation. If she failed to do this, or see her role in the matter, she would run the risk of being infected with the disease again herself.

She carefully and critically analysed the situation and made the following realisations:

- It is not my role to work out why he feels he has no sex life.

- It is not my duty to satisfy his sexual appetite even if he thinks it is – just like it is not his duty to satisfy mine.

- Sexual appetites can be satisfied through other means than just sex – through increased creativity and satisfaction with your own life.

Pleased with her analysis, she presented it to her husband. She then realised he was still suffering from the disease because of his response.

If you are curious to know how he responded, turn over the page.

Purposely left blank

Man's Stressful Wife

A man has had an unhappy, stress-ridden wife for many years. When he retired, he decided to help her and spent hours persuading her to take stress-management courses or relaxation seminars like the ones he used to take when working. Neither his ideas nor words of encouragement had any effect.

Then, one day, he noticed an advert for Tai Chi classes at the local village hall and convinced her to go along. After her first class, she came home full of vitality and announced that all her problems were solved. He was over the moon with joy and began to reap the benefits of a happy wife. He was glad to see that she practiced Tai Chi every morning at sunrise and every evening at sunset and looked forward to a long and rewarding retirement with his well-balanced wife.

After a couple of weeks, she doubled the frequency of her Tai Chi practice and after a month increased it further until she was doing ten minutes of Tai Chi every half an hour. No matter where they were or what they were doing: in the supermarket, at the doctors, walking in the park, his wife would stop every half an hour and do ten minutes of Tai Chi.

As time went on, he felt more and more irritated and embarrassed by her need to practice Tai Chi. When, in the park he would hide behind a tree, In the supermarket, he would switch isles and spend the time reading the labels on tins. At the doctor's, he would bury his head in "Home and Garden" or "Women's Realm" magazines.

One day, during her third 10-minute practice session in the High Street, he broke down and began sobbing like a child.

"What's the matter dear?" his wife asked calmly and lovingly. "I just can't cope!" he blubbered.

"Oh don't you worry, my darling. I know exactly what you need," she exclaimed with great enthusiasm, "Tai Chi!!"

The Doctor and his Pet Chimpanzee

Once there was a doctor who was not very popular with women. In primary school he was small, spectacled and a bit of a swat. He went through secondary school as the punch line of his classmate's jokes and never got close enough to a girl to sniff her perfume, let alone ask one out on a date.

Throughout his university life, he only had one friend - a biology student who had grown up on Born-Free and rat dissection. One day, this old friend, who was now a well-known biologist, working on significant research projects all over the world, asked him if he could look after Betty, his pet chimpanzee. The doctor was a bit apprehensive but nonetheless agreed.

As fate would have it, the friend who had, in fact, left on a two-week expedition to study wild cats in Africa, was ravaged by a lion and returned in a coffin. The doctor was informed and asked by the relatives if he would be so kind as to keep the chimpanzee for them. He hesitated only briefly this time, as he had grown very fond of the animal who lived in his flat in London and went everywhere with him.

One day, the chimpanzee was too eager to get to its adored baker's shop for a chocolate bun and ended up under the wheels of a truck. The doctor was devastated and went to great pains to arrange a church funeral for the animal. He eventually found undertakers who would take care of the body. The person in charge of the undertaker service was a woman. She was so touched by his concern for the chimpanzee that she fell in love with him.

Shortly after the funeral, they married and lived together in the doctor's flat in London. The doctor became very successful. Little by little, he suggested to his wife, that she stay at home. She needn't work now that his practice was so lucrative. She agreed.

As she grew older, she developed osteoporosis and he spent hours lovingly massaging her aching limbs. Her hair began to fall out and he bought her a wig to cover her balding scalp. It was a small 'short-back-and-sides' wig which was the only haircut he knew - a little unusual for a woman, but he thought she looked very attractive with it on.

His wife lived a solitary life. Every time she wanted to visit a friend, he would beg her to stay at home with him. Every time she wanted to go out alone, he begged to go with her. Every time people came to visit, he behaved in a very possessive way and scared them off.

She began to develop a speech impediment, struggling with her b's and p's. He didn't mind. He loved her dearly and helped her as best he could by saying the words for her. Soon she had problems pronouncing most consonants so that *How nice to meet you*, became h*ow ice oo eet you'*. This didn't bother him in the slightest - he simply helped her by completing her sentences.

The condition got worse still. Being a doctor, he felt it was his duty to try and help her and so prescribed some medicine he thought may help. It didn't. Things got worse and worse until all she could utter was *ow ee ou*.

The doctor continued to love her regardless and learned to understand what she was saying even though her vocabulary was so limited. As she grew older still, she became incontinent and he bought her nappies covered with frilly panties.

Her osteoporosis also worsened and she stooped and limped when she walked. When they went out together, she would limp behind him because she couldn't walk at his pace and was too proud to let him take her hand or carry her. One day whilst in the park, he saw a very innovative thing: a dog on a leash made of a nylon you could barely see. It enabled the dog to walk at heel without others noticing it was being led by the owner. He thought such a leash would make an ideal Christmas present and jumped inside at the thought of getting one with an engraving: *To my darling Betty.*

Dial S-T-R-E-S-S for Success

It was Stress Awareness Day today, or so it said on a leaflet a man rudely thrust into my hand as I rushed into Manchester station. I hoped to catch the 10:19 train to Sheffield. When I arrived at the platform, a polite, but firm female voice informed passengers that the train had been delayed by twenty minutes. I phoned my mother to let her know I'd be late.

When the twenty minutes were up, the same voice announced that the train had been cancelled. It was 10:40. We were referred to the 10:43 train on a different platform. I hurried there, determined to catch it. I arrived, all out of breath, hot and bothered, to the sound of another announcement: the 10:43 to Sheffield has been delayed by 15 minutes.

I rang my mother again. As soon as I hung up, the polite voice returned to let passengers know that the 10:43 to Sheffield had been delayed a further 25 minutes. I rang mother:
"Don't bother coming to pick me up. I'll call when I arrive.
This is hilarious," I added.
"No, it isn't. It's a bloody nuisance!" she replied. Mother didn't know that it was Stress Awareness Day.

Here in Manchester, Stress Awareness Day was in full swing. And British Rail was playing a major role in raising awareness of it - for free! Good that I had the leaflet telling me how to combat it. 'But don't forget,' it warns, 'this stress came from you. You were doing too much and didn't recognise it early enough to be able to do something about it!'

Thanks BR, thanks stress awareness campaigners, I thought cynically and imagined the knock-on effect the cancellation of this one train on this one day in the year could have: interviews missed, job opportunities lost, friends and loved ones stood up, annoyances, cancellations, divorces, even. And it all had a wonderful spin-off for the mobile phone industry. I had already made three telephone calls. All around me phones were ringing; one every minute, or there about. All those passengers having to tell someone of their delay; those someone's having to inform other affected parties about the delay and so on and so forth. Not quite ad infinitum, but enough extra calls to make a difference.

One train, one cancellation, one delay in one country, on one sunny day in October and the amount of stress awareness generated, let alone new patients, was quite substantial.

What an achievement! It deserves an award: a Duke of Edinburgh prize for a new business concept and enterprising conduct; for caring about people, practical, hands-on communication; for cunning and dedication and determination and, above all, success!

The Flute Player

Mike is 65 and driving north to Scotland, just his flute and himself, for his first, long-earned vacation since he went into retirement. After 35 years working as music teacher in a large secondary school south of London, he felt he needed the peace and beauty of the mountains, and is already dreaming of the inspiring, majestic highlands and hours of simply blowing his flute. Just outside Croydon, before he meets the junction with the M25 to head north, he sees the next traffic light in the distance turn red and begins to brake. He is still doing around 30km/h when a motorbike with sidecar veers in front of him and he has to suddenly slam on the brakes. The car doesn't come to a halt immediately but slides a few centimetres on and there is a little popping sound as his front bumper hits the sidecar.

The motorcyclist gestures to him to follow him off the main road and into a side road. Mike gets out and sees there is a tiny dent. He is about to speak when the motorcyclist charges at him, arms flailing.

"You fucking arsehole!" shouts a young male in his twenties. "Haven't you heard of brakes?"

Mike, flustered by the man's aggression, but keeping calm as his years of teaching rowdy teenagers had taught him, replies:

"Have you not heard of indicators?"

"I indicated about a mile ago. You blind, Grandpa?"

Pressing his lips together to repress an uncouth reply, Mike takes a deep breath and offers: "Listen, I admit it was my fault. Why not let's exchange address and telephone numbers and I'll sort it out with my insurance?"

"Not until I have an apology from you Grandpa."

"I'm sorry."

"No Granddaddy. That's not what I mean. You ram my arse. You lick my arse!" and he makes a move to unzip his trousers.

Mike makes a move towards his car, rummages in the glove compartment for paper and pen. The motorcyclist suddenly appears behind him "Come away from the car or I'll shoot!" his right hand holding what looks like a small revolver.

"Jesus!" Mike exclaims.

"No Jesus pops, just hell. Over here! Spread them! Now lie down and hand over the keys. Easy does it..."

Once he has the keys, he kicks Mike and cries:
"Ha! What a fucking idiot. Scared of a little toy gun are you? Poor Granddaddy." And he gleefully demonstrates that the gun is in fact a cigarette lighter.

Then everything went so fast it was difficult, if not impossible, to recount it in every detail to the police afterwards. The motorcyclist had the keys, then he didn't have them - he must have dropped them. Mike saw him fumbling for something on the floor and then, in a split second, Mike was up and heading towards his car. He grabbed his flute case which was on the passenger seat, took out the mouthpiece and slid it up his sleeve. The motorcyclist came running behind him, pulled him backwards out of the car and tried to get into the driver's seat. Mike regained his balance, and from inside his sleeve, pushed one end of the mouthpiece into the motorcyclist's back. "One more move and you're dead!" he shouted, and with a steady hand, pushed the barrel of the flute further and firmly into the man's backbone.

Into a Breath of Warm Air

Once upon a time, in a land where deer and bear roamed free in the forest and the only predator was man, a female wolf walked down the drive and into my back garden. On the night she came I was alone in the house, sitting as I often did, at the window, staring out into darkness. I kept still as she approached, for I was afraid.

She came up close, flashing her fangs, twitching her snout and spilling hot breath onto the cold glass between us. As the patch of condensation cleared, her eyes drilled deep into the pane; a black tunnel with a speck of brightness, beckoning me. I was reeled in: a fish caught on a minuscule hook of light.

A thousand sharp sounds reverberated in my ears as I crashed through. And as she galloped majestically away, I saw her mane-like hair dance in twirls above her head, her nostrils billow out wide and her hooves glint in the light of the moon. She was no ordinary wolf. She was a wondrous creature; part horse and part wolf. I called her Wolf-Mare.

She did not come again. Every night I waited for her. Every night, darkness dissolved into dawn and there was no sign of her. Perhaps it was just a dream. How I yearned to see the creature once more, dip into her eyes and feel their wild and infinite depth.

Months and years passed. I no longer sat at the window. I no longer waited, or hoped, or dreamed.

Then one autumn evening, when the sun had sunk behind the trees at the bottom of my garden and the evening mist was bringing in the night, I was drawn to the window by a familiar sight on the pane. I peered through the patch of condensation and when I did, thought I saw a round shape like a head and something jagged like teeth. I opened the window and strained to see through the milky night. I saw nothing; but my cheeks were caressed by a warm wind as soft and luxurious as silk.

My hands shook as they grabbed the window frame and heaved my body up onto the ledge. My legs, unsure of what to do, kicked aimlessly out into the night, loosening my weak grip, thrusting my body through the window and dropping me like a corpse onto the wet grass. I lay there for a long time, the warm wind stroking my face.

Nervously, I called out

'Wolf-Mare, are you there?'

There was no answer.

I sensed some movement and the wind blew harder.

I called out again:

'Who are you?'

And still there was no answer.

Yet I knew my creature was there: I could sense her presence and I could taste her sweet breath. I stood up, stepped into the gusty wind which was blasting out of the forest and called out again:

'Who are you?'

I ran, calling out repeatedly:

'Who are you?'

And the forest, thick with wild trees, echoed back:

'Who are you?'

I called louder still.

My voice taking off into the night and hurtling back at me with force:

WhoooooooooooaaaaareYyyyyyyyyou?

I ran faster, crying out continually in the direction of my echo. And as I did, my buttons flew off and bounced away with my clothes; the laces undid themselves and threw the shoes off my feet; the elastic snapped and released the underwear from my body; the pins jumped out of my hair tossing it down my bare back; my toes spread out, my feet grew large, my neck extended forwards and my nostrils widened. I dashed through the trees, head lunging ahead, nose sucking in the sweet, warm wind. And out of my throat came a bellow from the deepness of my soul.

IIIIIIIIIIIIIIIIIIIIIaaaammmmmYyyyyyou.

She

Once upon a time there was a rare and wondrous creature called 'She'. She had a black mane, shining fur, large, oval-shaped eyes and long ears that pointed skyward like a proud horse. Her nostrils were wide and her snout sharp and full of fangs like a hungry wolf. In fact, she was part horse, part wolf: a wolf-mare. She loved to gallop through the countryside and breathe in the sights and smells of nature. This was her home, the place where She was free to be who she wanted to be and where her many intuitive powers and instincts could be explored and developed in tune with the wilderness around her.

One fine day whilst She was frolicking through the meadows enjoying the manifold colours and scents of Spring, a warm wind from the South called out her name. 'She,' it called 'The time has come for you to go to the land of humans and recount your story of the wilderness. You are the lost feminine spirit and I call you to tell your story to the human world...'

She was delighted to be called by the wind and immediately thought of ways in which she could tell her story. She imagined its bright colours, its graceful movements, its beautiful sounds and delicious smells. She could hardly contain her excitement at the thought of completing this task and galloped all afternoon long.

When night fell, all became quiet and calm. She lay down with exhaustion in the moist grass and became pensive. The excitement of the day disappeared and she suddenly felt empty and alone. She wondered whether she had imagined the warm South wind and lowered her head with sorrow and shame. Perhaps she was not the creature she thought she was and would not tell her story.

Whilst these thoughts swam around her weary head, She caught a glimpse of something bright. She looked up and saw a speck of light peeping out from behind a thick cloud. As she watched and waited, the light became larger and rounder. It was the moon. Instinctively she raised her head and called up to it, as only a wolf knows how. And when she did, a figure appeared before her.

292

"My name is 'Mutter," said the figure, "I heard your call and have come to help you. I have brought you this gift," and she held out a small plant. It was a nettle with many young green leaves and clusters of blossoms as white as the light radiating off the moon figure herself. The wolf-mare took the nettle plant and held it close to her heart. Mutter spoke again:

"Pluck the blossoms from the plant and suck out the sweet nectar they contain. This will give you the strength you need to carry on your path. When you have drunk the juice of the blossoms, put the plant somewhere safe and leave it there. The leaves will grow large and sharp and will be your weapons. The edge of the leaf will become a tool to cut through your shackles and the tip of the leaf will be a weapon to ward off your enemy. When you have used them, the leaves will become limp and lose their power. Take the limp leaves and let your hot tears of pain drip over them to make an infusion. Drink this nettle infusion and you will be free to go wherever your heart desires."

She thanked Mutter for the gift and her heart sang with the same joy that it had felt in the morning after the south wind had spoken to her. And She set off on her way to tell her story to the human world, drinking with every step she made, the nectar from a blossom.

When She finally arrived at the gate that marked the border between her world and the human world, she had used up all the blossoms and hid the plant carefully away under her thick mane.

She pushed hard at the gate but it would not open. After a few moments, words colours and sounds gushed through her head making her dizzy and dazzled. She wondered whether the blossom nectar was really giving her strength. Perhaps it was poisonous. Perhaps there had never been a warm south wind and she was merely a crazy and lonely creature with nothing to say. Just as she thought these things, a cold wind came from the north and turned the night air a misty grey. Out of the dark cloud, a voice roared louder than any voice she had ever heard:

"Yes, that's exactly what you are. Just a crazy, lonely creature that has let herself be fooled. Blossoms giving you strength indeed! Fancy believing that. And as for thinking you are a feminine spirit with a story to tell - Who do you think you are? How dare you think you are something special. You're just a weak, pathetic, odd creature that no-one cares about."

She felt like running into the dark mist and attacking who or whatever was behind the voice but her legs remained still and lifeless on the ground. The voice became louder and louder:

"Go back to the woods where you belong. The human world has no place for you. You have no talent. You cannot paint or spell or think coherent thoughts. You are nothing but a strange unlovable creature. Go back to the forest and live your pathetic life to an end like all the other rejects. You are worthless and have nothing to say. How dare you think you do. I will show you what a nothing you are."

He then grabbed a rope and wound it round and round her body squeezing it tight. She bucked and darted and whinnied and howled but the more she struggled, the tighter the rope became. Finally, he attached a harness around her head and a muzzle around her snout and forced her to the ground.

She lay there, bound and gagged on the wet night grass and wished to die. Darkness prevailed, erasing all but one miniscule speck of light. That tiny speck of light stayed and stayed until She was compelled to open her eyes to see where it came from. When she did, she saw the moon. At once she remembered the plant hidden in her mane and struggled to reach it through the rope. She managed to pull one nettle leaf out and as the light of the moon shone down on it, it began to move to and fro in a sawing motion. Slowly at first and then faster and faster until the rope lay in shreds all around her. She stood up and darted to the gate.

"You cannot get through." the voice roared and a huge monster loomed in front of her. Without hesitating she took the leaf that had been her saw and hurled it at him. The leaf flew through the air like a silver dagger and hit the monster between the eyes. He screamed, lurched forwards with outstretched arms and tried to grab her but he was blinded by a fountain of hot tears that poured forth from his eyes and so failed to see where she was. She quickly ran past him to the gate and pushed at it with all her strength but still it would not open. The monster came lolloping over and roared with delight.

"Ha, you will never get through. The gate can only be opened by a voice as loud and mighty as mine."

Her throat was sore from the rope and when she tried to howl her great wolf's howl, a squeak was all that came out. She then remembered what Mutter had said about the tea. She retrieved the nettle leaves, placed them in her hoof and held it up to receive the hot tears from the monster's eyes. The leaves turned the water into a quenching nettle tea and she drank every last drop. Refreshed, her voice burst forth in the most tremendous song ever heard.

The gate swung open and she leapt through.

Peppermint Moment

It's the beginning of May and I leave the house at dawn in a flimsy nightdress to pick peppermint. In a while, I will make my first mint tea of the year with fresh leaves harvested from the plant. It grows between the sage and lemon balm, equidistant from my house and a feisty brook hidden from sight, but not sound, by some evergreens.

I take off my slippers and walk barefoot along the ribbed wood of the balcony to the spiral staircase which connects my house to the garden below. With each step the sole of my foot winces as the wood-grooves pinch the skin. Goosebumps creep up my legs to my knees. I continue down the stairs, half asleep and reluctant to wake up. My eyes are gritty from the night and my legs, stiff from their long rest, need coaxing to walk.

*

It's been six months since I drank peppermint tea and just as long since I wrote some creative prose. I used to write pieces regularly. I was in touch with my senses then. No, more than that, I was in touch with my soul. Now I wonder where it is. It appears to have left me – or someone or something has stolen it.

For many nights I have been asking for a dream to come and show me the way back to it. All through winter, dreams have stayed away. I have looked for inspiration in myths, stories and poems. I have listened to other people's advice. Yet, day after day I have woken to a dry heart and blank page. Each morning I have cursed the night for not giving me ideas. I have scratched my head and knocked loudly on my hard skull. All this fuss has woken up my inner critic, a persistent enemy of mine. His tongue has wrapped itself tight around my writer's wrist and holds my hand whenever it takes the pen: *What's the use of words when there are children starving? What will prose do to stop wars, feed babies bellies and heal the world?* I have no answers. These are questions for the soul, not the mind. My rational tongue may talk reason and logic to the critic and make him quiet for a while, but the grasp on my wrist does not loosen.

*

At the bottom of the stairs, I hesitate before I put a foot onto the patio. The stones, though smoother than the wood, are colder, and my toes curl at the change in temperature. Just a few steps and I am at the edge of the lawn. I know the grass is wet – not from a rain shower, but from heavy dew. I hesitate at the edge of the patio like one does at the edge of a cold sea before taking the plunge. My lawn is emerald green in this light and bobbing over the surface are a thousand and more white daisy heads, still round and closed from the night. Green blades of grass eagerly lick between my toes as I move.

I crouch down. The peppermint season is young and slow in showing progress above ground. The six or less dark green leaves on each short stem are wrinkled and downy with newness. I carefully snap off a peppermint shoot, shake a resident ant out, wipe cuckoo spittle from the nodes and place the harvest in my hand. I cup my palm to protect the peppermint and walk back to the patio like one might wade through the sea. The lawn is my ocean and I am a vessel bringing in the peppermint. My cupped palm is the deck and my body the mast, my nightie the sail and my head the crow's nest steering me back to the harbour. I greet the seagulls, looking up to the sky to them and calling out, "'Tis a great day for fishing," and their wings flap up in graceful, wide smiles. I lay anchor close to shore, vow to return again tomorrow and set foot on dry land. The ground feels firmer than on the outward journey for all the rocking movements of the sea I have experienced and I rejoice to be back. I merrily make my way to the house, my mint - catch of the day – lying patiently and calm in my hand. I enter the house and prepare my drink. It's after sunrise, yet not quite morning. I go inside and the seagull sound can no longer be heard. All is still except for wood pigeon's soothing coo coo coo, coo coo. Coo coo coo, coo coo.

I put the peppermint leaves in a porcelain cup and pour boiling water over them. I sip the liquid and grasp the pen. My wrist loosens and the nib begins to make marks across the page. A leaf slips out of the cup as I drink and lands on my tongue. It feels weightless. I press it gently to the roof of my mouth and hold it there, closing my eyes.

Mint flavour slithers over my taste buds, down the inside of my throat and into my body, criss-crossing up and down my spine, stroking it with the smooth skin of a sea snake in a swirling dance. I am suddenly back on the ship, sailing once more across my green ocean decorated with daisy-coloured buoys, over to the peppermint. Dozens of fish are flipping up and splashing on the surface, asking to be caught. All have scales that shine ruby, emerald and diamond in the sun. And then the line tugs hard and I hold on strong, burning my palms. The catch is too powerful for me to fish out and so I let go. The line dances away, taking ten metres into the deep waters. I grab hold of the end of the rod at the last minute and am yanked over the side, down with the fish, into the sea, on and on. I can see the creature ahead, flying like a bird with the golden wings of a phoenix and the long tail of a serpent. It soars past rocks and corals, past turtles and hairy sea slugs, to beyond.

I realise I am the fish's catch. All is dark and there is no more air to breathe. Water gushes in, filling my veins and cells, washing all human matter out and replacing it with new waters.

I am neither alive, nor dead, neither man nor fish, neither in this world nor the next. I am in-between – in human imagination - where mind and soul can meet. It is a place in which time, past present and future dance together, where all living creatures who have long left this world are living new lives and where all stories ever to be written are contained in a giant pot into which I may dip my writing pen and fill it to the brim with ink that never runs out. And I realise that the mint is teaching me about the true essence of life: the moment of creation; a moment in which there is a still point, when all is quiet and the world is linked by invisible strands. Each strand is like a fishing line and I, the fisherman, can go out and cast the thread and fish out anything and everything ever imagined. – which is infinite. And the pot is bottomless, timeless and ageless and has always been there, at my service, without me making use of it. Above all, I have not made use of it to create peace.

All of this comes through the essence of peppermint and a pen filled with the kind of ink it creates, drunk from that pool. And the words are the fish that land on the page – pieces of prose which eventually make an entire text: one which has not been thought up by a rational human mind, but which comes from the soul: eternal and everlasting.

Horse Power

My dad has a motorbike. He loves it because it has lots of what he calls horsepower. I'm not sure what he means; he's not so keen on horses. In the summer, he often rides past a field where there are two black workhorses and if the farmer is there, he raises his fist at my dad and shouts. I asked Dad what the farmer is saying and he said that he is probably saying 'Don't frighten the horses'. I laughed because my dad only zooms past the horse's field because he is scared they might break free and knock him off his bike. 'That's ironic.' says my dad. I don't know what ironic means. I just think it's funny.

Dad's motorbike drinks gallons of thick golden petrol. I like to watch him pour it in and listen to the glugging sound it makes. I practiced doing the same with my soup during tea and asked for extra portions so that I could get the sound just right. My mum was watching me with a deep frown on her face and said, in a cross voice, that I was eating like a pig and then, in a less cross voice, that I might be growing and was eating like a horse. I didn't care whether I was a pig or horse. I was just glad that I sounded like Dad's motorbike.

When cold weather comes, Dad goes out on his motorbike less and less. He spends a lot of time in the garage cleaning and polishing the bike with wax and a soft leather cloth. He then drapes a woolen blanket over it so that the engine keeps warm and the dust doesn't get into the parts. Every day before he goes to work, he looks at the thermometer outside. If the red liquid inside the thermometer is below number 10, it's too cold to take the bike. Dad says it's not good for the sinuses. I agreed; you can't see the signs so easily when it is frosty. Dad insists that it's his nose he's worried about, not his eyes. Anyway, this morning he came in beaming and so I knew that the thermometer had given him permission to go on the motorbike. During breakfast, Mum and Dad were having a grown-up discussion. I wasn't listening until Mum said something about changing horses in midstream. I wondered what she meant and when I saw Dad's face become sad, I knew that it had something to do with the motorbike. Dad said he had to take the car because he'd promised to pick up some groceries on the way home. Dad explained that changing horses in midstream just meant changing your plan in the middle of it. I think Dad is wrong. Changing horses in midstream means having to take the car instead of the motorbike.

I know that spring has arrived when the daffodils are out and Dad lifts the blanket off his motorbike. The metal shines like armor and the blue paint is as deep and beautiful as the sea. I know the motorbike is happy when Dad takes off its winter coat and strokes the seat, because it smiles at me. Dad says it is only my reflection in the chrome, but I think the motorbike really can smile. I wanted my bike to smile too and so I polished it up nice and bright. I told Pete, our next door neighbour that I have a bike like my dad's. He didn't believe me and when I showed him my pushbike all sparkling like my dad's motorbike, he said that mine was a horse of another colour. I thought about it and realised that he was right: my bike is red, and will never be sea-blue like my dad's.

Mum has said that if I continue to grow as fast as I have been doing, I will need a new bike. Now I know what colour I shall wish for.

After the long winter in the garage, the engine is too cold to start straight away. Dad has to push with all his might to get the bike to the top of our drive, climb on and then let it roll down as fast as possible. If he's lucky, the engine will bump into life first try. If not, he has to keep on trying until he's exhausted. Mum says he's flogging a dead horse, but I know that Dad's motorbike will eventually start roaring. When it does, my heart dances and my legs go all wobbly with excitement. Now I know what the horses feel like when they are finally let out of the stable after the long winter. Dad calls it frisky and it's what he's frightened of.

Dad keeps on correcting me when I call the smoke coming from the pipes at the back 'perfume'. He says it's exhaust fume not perfume. It's extremely poisonous and you shouldn't breathe it in. Mum tells Dad off for getting on his high horse about it.

I think that they both talk a load of rubbish. Dad is only on his high horse when he has his leather gear on, is wearing his Darth-Vader helmet and sits on his motorbike full of horse power.

Enough to make a Cat Laugh

We have new neighbours, a family of four, and I have made friends with Kitty.

She has an odd way of talking which I don't always understand. She says it's because her mum's French and grew up in Irish-America and her dad's American and grew up in Australian-England. My mum says I may have it all cross-wired. I don't know what she means. I just think I may have got it wrong.

Her brother is fifteen, is called Tom and is a 'mind-my-French bastard' like all older brothers are, says Kitty. I wouldn't know, I can't speak French and am an only child.

What I do know is that they have a house full of cats. They have a 'cheshire cat' who apparently smiles a lot and a 'kilkenny cat' who likes to fight, plus another breed of cat I didn't catch the name of. Then there's 'bell' the cat (which mum says is probably spelled 'Belle' like the French word for beautiful), 'catty' (who is Kitty's cat I think) and Tom (no prizes for guessing whose cat that is). They also have at least half a dozen baby cats it seems, with plenty more on the way: only yesterday at the playground, Kitty mentioned that her parents were having kittens.

I think it's funny the way she talks about the cats as if they were little babies, and all the strange things they do to care for them like, for example, they dust kittens, they even have a cat's cradle, put on cat's pyjamas, hold cat concerts for them, go on cat walks and have devised a special cat call, when they are out at night.

Having said that, Kitty's brother, who she keeps on saying is in the middle of "add o' less cents" (which must be some kind of Irish-American game) doesn't seem to be half as kind to his cat. She told me that he's put the cat among the pigeons several times and I guess that's really cruel because the birds probably peck at the cat's eyes. Kitty also said that he claims his room in the new house isn't big enough to swing a cat in, and I wonder how he knows.

I do think Kitty exaggerates sometimes though, because she went on to say that when their mum and dad wouldn't let him have a bigger room, he turned the cat in the pan because he wanted to see how the cat jumps, but apparently made a dog's dinner out of it

302

instead. According to Kitty, Tom has done all sorts of other nasty things including: singe, skin and whip the cat.

Of course, I have no way of knowing: I have never had a brother or a cat, but I told her that I'd overheard grownups talking about brothers and sisters doing crazy things for attention. I wouldn't have told her if I'd known she would tell-tale. The next day she came running up to me in the playground and said that what I had said, had made him shoot the cat.

I was really upset that I may have caused the poor cat to die and then realised that if he had really shot the cat, I would have heard it, because their house is attached to ours. Now, I'm not sure she's telling the truth. I don't like people lying to me and I told her so. She pushed me into the sandpit and ran off.

The next day, I went around to her house to ask if she could play; I was bored because there are no other children on our street. Her brother answered the door and said that she couldn't because the cat had got her tongue. I told him that he was a mean bastard just like Kitty said he was. He shouted at me and I screamed louder than I had ever done before. But he just put his hands over his ears and kept on repeating, suffering cats, suffering cats, over and over again.

Later, when I had calmed down, I told Mum and Dad all about the cat-torturer next-door. They agreed to go around to Kitty's house with me to see what was going on, but made me promise not to accuse anyone of anything until we had some hard evidence.

Kitty's mum answered the door and let us in. She was suspiciously friendly, saying she was thrilled to meet us and there was nothing better than good neighbourly relations. She said we must stay for some tea and freshly baked cake. When we arrived in the kitchen, she went over to boil the kettle and, as she did, pointed to the hob and said it was the cat's whiskers. I was horrified and nudged Mum so that she would say something. She just kept on looking at the place where the whiskers were probably lying, all frazzled. No doubt she would try and take a sample when Kitty's mum wasn't looking.

Dad didn't seem to have noticed anything at all and in exasperation, I pulled him to one side and whispered that this was where Tom must have done all those nasty things to the cat. He whispered back, 'There's more than one way to skin a cat!' which was a bit puzzling but I think he was on to something. Mum, too, because she was now asking all sorts of questions about the different kitchen appliances, particularly the fridge. Kitty's mum opened it and exclaimed, 'Dog my cats, all the milk's gone!'.

I grabbed Dad's hand and hurried over to get a good look inside. Kitty's mum laughed and said that having hungry kittens in the house really didn't give you a cat-in-hell chance of keeping it stocked up. I stared at Mum and Dad, open-mouthed. They ignored me and unashamedly laughed along with the cat killer's mum. Whilst the tea was brewing, Kitty's mum took us on a tour of the house. There was not a single sign of a cat or kitten. This meant that a) they had been hidden away or b) they were all dead: murdered.

The last room Kitty's mum took us to was the playroom. On opening the door, she exclaimed, "There she is, looking like the cat who swallowed the canary!" I gasped and searched desperately for some support from Mum and Dad. They just laughed again. I was not only furious with them, but also very upset about the canary and confused about what I saw on entering the room: Kitty was playing with a beige-coloured puppy dog who she introduced as 'Catkins'.

Kitty's mum chuckled and said, "We nearly had kittens when she wanted to call it Kitty-Cat, so we compromised with 'Catkins.'"

"But," I stammered, looking at Kitty and then at her mum, "Where are all the cats?" "Cats?" she asked puzzled. "No cats live here - we're allergic to them. If Kitty's birthday present hadn't arrived this morning, though, we'd have been in the dog house, if you'll excuse the pun."

"Dog house?" I said baffled. "And what's a pun?"

Then they 'let the cat out of the bag' and I 'walked the cat back,' and we all burst out in raucous fits of giggles.

"Enough to make a cat laugh!" said Tom.

Dear Reader,

I have been feeling shattered ever since I watched the terrorist attack on television; ever since I saw the planes flying through floors 93-99 on 9/11; ever since I saw the Twin Towers crumbling like they were sandcastles; ever since I saw people jump out of windows and off rooftops without parachutes, even though they knew there was nothing below to catch them, nothing to keep them from the impact and certain death.

I felt like I was falling with them, rubble, dust and all; as if I was splattering on the ground; as if I was being buried alive by tons of debris. Yet, here I was in front of the screen, in real time, just like the scenes I was seeing. I did collapse. But it was inward, invisible. I crumpled, became discombobulated and crazed with fright. I was here but in an altered state – one I had been in during a nervous breakdown a few years before.

As soon as I regained some stability, I felt compelled to write. After I had written, I felt compelled to share it and sent my message out as an email to friends and acquaintances. It received a variety of responses. Many did not share my point of view, but many did. That was not the point. I just needed to feel that I was not alone. I think that a fellow writer was right when she wrote back: "I am very doubtful that people will be able to set aside thoughts of revenge in order to take as broad a view as you are trying to, though I fervently hope they will." And it was this kind of hope that motivated me to stand up and hold a speech at the Creative Writer's Club of Luxembourg during the monthly meeting on 9/12.

Dear Reader, you cannot imagine how sick I have been feeling ever since. In my speech, I admitted that I had a kamikaze pilot inside me that could lead to my own destruction if I didn't take care, and responsibility for it. I admitted that I suppress and repress feelings, betray myself, manipulate and blame others and the world at large for things that go wrong. I said that September 11th was a wake-up call for all of us; that we had not just been snoozing, but comatose. I said that our system had gone drastically wrong; that we are spending unforgivable amounts of energy and money on conniving, squabbling, comparing and striving to win, get ahead and beat others to goalposts that only exist in our egoic minds. I said that we were all to blame for this terrorist attack, that the aspect of us that is capable of such well-orchestrated acts of destruction as we saw in New York on Tuesday September 11th 2001, needs everybody's attention. It is not about finding 'them', the culprits, those monsters and getting rid of them, thinking we are thus eradicating the problem. As painful as it is to accept and embrace, terrorism will only be eradicated when we address our own inner terrorists; when we recognise the harm we cause ourselves and others whenever we judge, suppress, rage and hate. I said that understanding and balancing out the destructive and creative forces that live in every human being may be what our existence is all about; that it is an arduous task, yet possibly the only way to go forward in the aftermath of this terrorist attack. I said that we could learn from such horrors and it is our obligation to seriously look at the kind of example we are setting, what kind of role models we are for our children – for the future of mankind.

At the Creative Writer's Club, my speech landed on deaf ears. Only one (a New Yorker, actually) shared my point of view though he did not voice this publicly in the room but later, privately, in an email.

I have since received some wonderful messages from like-minded people. This gives me less of a feeling that I am an alien stuck out in the middle of nowhere with all of this. I did feel alone - not with my emotional reaction because I saw it in others around me and on the television - but with my thoughts and feelings that were largely unwelcome and that isolated me.

As we all move through the grief and pain and hurt that has been caused, I would like to trust that fertile ground for new direction and growth will emerge. I would further like to trust that forces will come into play such that may help us move beyond our limiting egos and personalities, into our higher self.

A force that is greater than me seems to be willing me to pass this message on. Thank you, dear Reader, for reading it.

ITALIANO

Andiamo in Italia

Non dimenticherò mai il giorno del nostro trasloco dal Lussemburgo in Italia, neanche il benvenuto che ci ha dato il nostro futuro paese al momento dell' arrivo. È stato il 22 dicembre, poco prima di natale.

Al mattino abbiamo salutato i nostri amici, i vicini e Schrassig, il piccolo paese a sud-est della capitale di Lussemburgo dove abbiamo vissuto negli ultimi quindici anni. Io ero molto triste. Ho pianto. Dopo tanti anni consideravamo il Lussemburgo come la nostra patria. Conoscevamo tanta gente. I nostri due figli ci erano nati. Dato che è una nazione multilingue dove vivono oltre ai lussemburghesi, molte persone di nationalità diversa, e che la nostra è una famiglia tedesco-inglese, il Lussemburgo era per noi un paese ideale. Non parlavamo ancora l'Italiano. Non conoscevamo l'Italia. Il trasloco era un passo nell' ignoto.

Come me, anche i miei figli si sentivano tristi al momento della partenza - sarebbe stato un cambiamento grandissimo: nuova abitazione, nuova scuola, nuova lingua, nuovi amici (e non sapevano se l'Italia gli sarebbe piaciuta). Per questo, mio marito ed io ritenevamo importantissimo che i nostri figli partecipassero alle discussione prima di prendere la decisione finale di lasciare il loro paese natale. Era una decisione di tutta la famiglia e non solo dei genitori.

Perciò, in giugno, sei mese prima del nostro trasferimento, abbiamo visitato Varese. Volevamo farci un' idea della città e della provincia. Siamo partiti nelle prime ore del mattino e arrivati alle due del pomeriggio in centro a Varese. Era un giorno caldissimo. Non c'era vento. I negozi erano chiusi e non c'era nessuno in città. Io ero molto delusa: Non era la città che mi aspettavo.

Visto che faceva così caldo abbiamo deciso di andare al lago di Varese a fare il bagno. Arrivati al lago abbiamo subito capito che non si faceva il bagno nel lago di Varese! I ragazzi erano molto scontenti. La delusione era completta.

Alla fine abbiamo trovato una spiaggia sul Lago Maggiore. L'acqua era buonissima, la vista splendida, l'aria fresca e dopo esserci rinfrescati, potevamo riconsiderare la situazione. Abbiamo perciò parlato dell' opportunità di crescere, di conoscere un' altra cultura, di imparare una lingua in più, di fare delle attività sportive diverse come lo sci, la vela...

Qualche settimana più tardi eravamo tutti d'accordo - andiamo in Italia!

La notte del nostro arrivo era serena, le montagne innevate scintillavano, le stelle luccicavano. Ogni paese era decorato con tantissime lampadine splendenti. Dopo 700 km di strada siamo arrivati a Besozzo, vicino a Brebbia, la nostra destinazione e d'ora in poi, il nostro nuovo paese. Anche qui c'erano delle illuminazioni di Natale: circa ogni 25 metri, la parola «Auguri» scritta con luce bianche, era sospesa in alto sulla strada sopra di noi - come se l'Italia ci volessi dare un gran benvenuto. Mi riempiva di gioia. Era il momento in cui io ero sicura che la nostra decisione di traslocare è stata giusta.

Regali del Passato

Quest' anno è stato il quarantacinquesimo natale della mia vita. Del mio primo, secondo, terzo e anche del mio quarto Natale, non ho nessun ricordo. E normale, penso. Ero troppo piccola. E degli altri quarantuno? I miei ricordi sono frammentari – non come delle finestre fracassate e irreparabili - ma piuttosto come centinaia di immagini sparse sul fondo del mio civello.

Quando vedo, sento o annuso qualsiasi cosa che è invisibilmente collegata a una esperienza legata al natale del passato, mi vengono presentate dalla mente parecchie immagini - non dissimili a fotografie di un album. Queste immagini non rimangono sulla pagina però, prendano vita e mi trasportano indietro nel tempo per rivivere nel presente, momenti e sentimenti di tempi passati.

Basta sentire la canzone 'Merry Christmas Everybody' del gruppo inglese 'Slade' e sono subito nel 1974 in Inghilterra. Porto un paio di *hot pants* rosse che mi ha appena regalato la mia madrina e mi sento grande anche se ho soltanto 9 anni e credo ancora a Babbo Natale. Le mie sorelle ed io stiamo preparando un pasto per Babbo Natale che consiste in un *Mince Pie* (tortina ripiena di mele, frutta secca e spezie) e un bicchiere di *Sherry*. Per Rudolf, la sua renna, offriamo (come sempre) una carota. Siamo sicure che la mattina dopo ci saranno delle briciole e una spolverata di paillettes: per noi delle prove tangibili che Babbo Natale esiste e che davvero scende dal camino con il suo gran sacco di regali. Sopratutto, sento la magia pura che porta questo periodo con sé e l'innocenza semplice della mia infanzia.

Il profumo di cannella mi riporto al natale trascorso in Germania nel 1982. Sto vendendo oli essenziali, sciarpe colorate e candele profumate al mercatino di Natale nel paese in cui abito con mia zia. Per tutta la giornata l'aria intorno a me è satura di fragranze diverse del cibo, delle bevande e dei prodotti tipici di quei giorni di festa. Dominante è il profumo di cannella. Mi sento quasi adulta e sono orgoliosa che riesco a parlare e lavorare in lingua tedesco.

A primavera, vedendo i primi fiori del ciliegio, faccio di nuovo un viaggio automatico nel passato. Questa volta torno negli Stati Uniti al Natale del 1985. Sto davanti alla Casa Bianca a Washington D.C guardando una meraviglia: dapertutto in città gli alberi sono in piena fioritura. Ci sono 22 gradi e i giornali parlano dell' "Estate di San Martino". Sono felicissima, inammorata di un ragazzo inglese che sta studiando per sei mesi all' università lì e non vedo l'ora di andare a New York nel Gennaio del 1986.

Nel mio garage ci sono al meno cinquanta scatole vuote e piegate rimaste dall' ultimo trasloco che mi fanno ritornare a diversi tempi, diversi paesi e diverse città – tanto sono stati i nostri traslochi. Le scatole ingombrano il garage. Mi domando perchè non le butto via. Non ne abbiamo più bisogno - allora sono inutile - come tante cose che ingombrano la casa. Ma le lascio. Chissà? Forse, un giorno ne avrò bisogno.

La memoria fa la stessa cosa coi nostri ricordi - anche se non tutti sono belli e qualcuno ci ingombra il civello; tuttavia ci danno la possibilità di viaggiare nel passato e goderci momenti del passato più e più volte ancora. Sono momenti di gioia, di pace e sopratutto momenti in cui sento dal fondo del cuore che c'è tanto di buono e di armonioso nel mondo – questo è un vero regalo di natale.

L' Estate del Duemillasette

Ogni giorno dalle otto della mattina alle otto della sera ero in contatto con l'argilla. Lavoravo nello studio di ceramica con altre otto partecipanti di un corso di scultura figurativa basato sulla forma della donna.

Eravamo tutti attenti, ascoltavamo, sperimentavamo. Di tanto in tanto chiacchieravamo, scambiavamo idee, ci incoraggiavamo, ci facevamo complimenti.

C'era sempre un po' di vento nello studio a causa di finestre e porte apperte. Talvolta entrava il gatto, Pico. A lui piaceva dormire sulla mensola. Altre volte arrivava il cane, Ciarli. A lui piaceva giocare con il ramo che portava in bocca. Avevamo sempre tempo per accarezzarli o giocare con loro.

Mentre modellavo, ho reflettuto sulla forma della donna: le curve del corpo, la morbidezza della pelle, la rotondità del seno, del sedere; il suo aspetto molle, docile, fragile, come l'argilla non cotta; il suo aspetto forte, resistente e finito, come l'argilla cotta.

Mi faceva molto piacere toccare il materiale, sentire l'humidità fresca della terra tra le mani: una sensazione calmante, rassicurante e potente.

Lavorando con la terra riuscivo a credere, senza dubbio, che siamo tutti fatti a mano – individui unici e creativi.

Sono tornata a casa con molto di più che mi aspettavo: tre sculture, l'amore per la Terra e l'impressione di capire un po' meglio l'umiltà, la simplicità e la bellezza della donna, della vita; di essere viva.

Due Bambini e un Gatto

In centro villaggio nel paese 'Pricewell' al nord di Inghilterra si trovava un piccolo negozio di articoli da regalo. La negoziante, signora Meanbody era una sessantenne severa e senza umore. I prezzi dei suoi 'regali' erano altissimi. "Tutto ciò che vendo in questa bottega è fatto a mano e unico nel mondo," giustificava lei quando un cliente metteva in dubbio i suoi prezzi. Che le sue parole fossero vere è poco probabile, ma la gente comperava comunque: magari piaceva a loro l'idea di possedere o regalare qualcosa di 'unico nel mondo'.

L'articolo più conveniente in questo negozio fu una statuetta in porcellana intitolata "Due Bambini e un Gatto". Come il titolo già indica l'oggetto era composto da due bambini e solo un gatto. I bambini erano seduti fianco a fianco su una panchina – l'uno con in grembo il gatto (che accarezzava), l'altro a mani vuote e uno sguardo pieno di tristezza e invidia. La signora Meanbody tenne il pezzo per un anno nella vetrina ma l'articolo non si vendeva e per questo abbassò il prezzo e mise l'oggetto su una mensola in un angolo buio, lontano dalla luce del giorno e dalle occhiate dei clienti che frequentavano il negozio.

Durante dieci anni la signora Meanbody aveva messo su questa mensola in totale 13 articoli 'invendibili'. Secondo lei, non valeva la pena tenere questo angolo del negozio pulito o spendere un soldo per illuminarlo.

Quello che non sapeva era che proprio quegli articoli 'invendibili' fossero unici nel mondo e inestimabili - non per la bellezza o per materiale di valore che poteva avere utilizzato il loro creatore, ma per il fatto che erano oggetti magici – avevano la capacità di parlare.

La sera, quando il negozio era chiuso e silenzioso, gli articoli da regalo nell' angolo buio del negozio cominciavano a bisbigliare, a ridere, a cantare. C'era solo uno che piangeva - sempre: il bambino senza gatto. Si lamentava in modo ininterrotto: "Vorrei che fosse io ad accarezzare il gatto. Vorrei che fosse io..." Gli altri articoli, stufi dei suoi lamenti rispondevano con crescente irritabilità: "Tu sei stato fatto come tu sei stato fatto e basta. Smettila! Non si possono cambiare le cose o volere l'impossibile. Allora piantala! Il meglio che si possa sperare è che un giorno venga un cliente, ti compri, ti metta sulla mensola a casa sua e ogni tanto ti dia delle carezze coi suoi occhi!"

Ma la notte seguente dalla sera alle sei quando la signora chiuse il negozio, fino alla mattina alle otto quando arrivò, il bambino senza gatto piangeva lo stesso.

Ogni anno durante il periodo di natale la signora Meanbody aveva bisogno di aiuto. Per risparmiare prendeva un giovane del villaggio e solo per un giorno alla settimana, il sabato. Quell' anno la sua assistente conveniente fu Emma, una regazza di sedici anni chi negli ultimi anni aveva comperato tre animali in porcellana dalla signora Meanbody: ciascuno era un regalo per se stessa il giorno del proprio compleanno. Aveva "L'Elefante con un Nodo nel Tronco", "Due Delfini Ingarbugliati in una Rete" e "Il Gatto Stregato" (a pelo rosso con delle macchie azzurre) - acquisti molto particolari, ognuno trovato nell' angolo buio.

Sabato – il giorno dell' orario continuato – la signora Meanbody traeva profitto dalla presenza di Emma per pranzare a lungo in un ristorante. Perciò da mezzogiorno fino alle due del pomeriggio, Emma era sempre da sola. Se non c'erano clienti trascorreva il tempo nell' angolo buio esaminando gli articoli 'invendibili'. Accendeva la luce, prendeva gli oggetti uno dopo l'altro in mano, li spolverava e li rimetteva con affezione ai loro posti. A lei dispiaceva tanto che nonostante i prezzi abbassati degli oggetti nell' angolo buio non ci fosse uno che avrebbe potuto permettersi. Aveva bisogno di tutti suoi soldi per regalare a sua madre che aveva il cancro, dei trattamenti che non pagava la cassa di malattia. Se avesse avuto più soldi però avrebbe comperato "Due Bambini e un Gatto" – non perché era il più conveniente di tutti, ma perché il bambino senza gatto dava l'impressione che avesse bisogno delle sue carezze.

Prese la statuetta in mano, passò le dita sopra il capo del bambino triste e lo baciò sulla guancia. "Ti capisco," disse a voce bassa, "Al posto tuo, anche io vorrei che fosse io col gatto." Emma stava proprio sul punto di rimettere "Due Bambini e un Gatto" sulla mensola quando entrò furibonda la Signora Meanbody: "Cosa diavolo stai facendo?" esclamò e tentò di prendere l'oggetto. Emma

315

lo tenne stretto tra le braccia ma la signora Meanbody divenne isterica, l'attaccò. La statuetta cadde a terra, e si spaccò. La meschina Signora Meanbody gridò, "Adesso voglio che tu raccolga i pezzi, mi dia i soldi per il danno e lasci subito il mio negozio." Emma obbedì, se ne andò e quella notte pianse tutte le sue lacrime.

Il giorno dopo si mise a ripararlo. Non era facile: c'erano mille pezzetini da incollare e mancavano anche alcuni che erano per sempre persi nel negozio della signora Meanbody dove Emma non avrebbe mai più avuto voglia di ritornare. Lavorò tutta la domenica e a mezzanotte incollò l'ultimo frammento. Ammirò il risultato. Le fece venire le lacrime agli occhi – questa volta per felicità. Dopo la riperazione, vedendo che era rimasta una fessura grande nelle coscie del bambino senza gatto, Emma aveva messo "Il Gatto Stregato" per coprire la parte danneggiata. Andò benissimo. Il bambino, una volta senza gatto, teneva adesso in grembo veramente il gatto a pelo rosso con delle macchie azzurre. A Emma sembrava che anche lo sguardo triste e invidioso di prima fosse sparito. "Ormai non devi piangere più, caro," disse al bambino.

Contentissima lo mise sulla mensola accanto agli altri oggetti magici e inestimabili e disse: "Domani parlerò con Signor Goodman. Lui sa bene il vostro valore e conosce collezionisti che pagheranno i prezzi guisti per voi. Ma tu, Due Bambini e Due Gatti, tu puoi stare per sempre qui da me."

Il Mio Più Caro Amico

La mattina del mio primo giorno di scuola primaria ero contentissima che finalmente era arrivata l'ora di vestirmi in modo identico alle mie sorelle più grandi. La divisa obligatoria della scuola era composta di una gonna, un maglione e un cappellino tutto in azzurro scuro e una camicia bianca.

Rimasi fermo davanti allo specchio per molto tempo. Come mi piaceva quella bambina – sembrava una vera scolara! Non vedevo l'ora di portare a casa qualche libro scolastico, dei compiti importanti e vedere incollata nel mio quaderno una stellina colore d'oro come quelle che avevo visto sui quaderni delle mie sorelle.

Prima di uscire salii per un'ultima volta per mostrare il mio nuovo *look* a Sky – il mio peluche preferito, un cane color cielo. 'Cosa ne pensi, Sky?' gli chiesi e lo presi in braccio raccontandogli come ero triste di doverlo lasciare a casa fino al mio ritorno dalla scuola. Anche se a cinque anni mi sentivo già grande e pronta per la vita scolastica, non potevo ancora imaginare di stare tutta una giornata senza di lui. Sky mi ascoltava e mi diceva di non preoccuparmi. Aveva sempre un buon consiglio e mi aiutava a superare ogni difficoltà nella mia vita. Era il mio più caro amico del mondo.

La sua pelliccia era così morbida che non potevo resistere ad accarezarlo ad ogni occasione... Avendo lo avuto per quasi 4 anni ce n'erano state tantissime carezze. Il suo pelo era diventato abbastanzo rado. In verità, Sky si stava scucendo. Mia mamma l'aveva rammendato una dozina di volte però il tissuto non teneva più a lungo e quindi si trovava l'impagliatura di Sky ovunque.

Il mio primo giorno di scuola andò benissimo. Mia mamma mi aspettava davanti al cancello all'uscita da scuola e mi accompagnò a casa. Quando arrivammo, salii subito nella mia camera per raccontare tutto a Sky. Non c'era sul letto dove pensavo di averlo lasciato quella mattina. Cercai in bagno – forse l'avevo con me mentre mi lavavo i denti, pensai. Ma non c'era neanche lì. Scesi per chiedere a mia mamma. Stava preparando la cena. 'Dov'è Sky?' Mia mamma esitò poi disse con voce dolce, 'Mi dispiace tantissimo ma Sky era troppo logoro per tenerlo ancora e per questo l'ho dovuto buttare via.   L'impagliatura, sai … ' Non ascoltavo più, andavo in direzione del bidone della spazzatura. Mamma mi fermò. 'Il spazzino ha già fatto la raccolta rifiuti.'

La Luna e L'Amore

Dalla sua posizione in alto nel cielo, la luna poteva osservare molto bene tutto ciò che succedeva sulla Terra, soprattutto durante le notti in cui il suo volto era tondo e risplendente. I suoi lunghi raggi di luce bianca arrivavano fino alle sponde di tutti i laghi e alle coste di tutti i mari che si trovavano nel suo emisfero.

Da un' eternità la luna illuminava la Terra di notte e si divertiva a guardare l'effetto positivo che aveva sugli animali, sugli uccelli, e sulla gente. Le sue notti preferite erano quelle più calde nei mesi d'estate: era durante questo periodo che si incontravano gli innamorati. La luna non si stancava mai di osservare come si abbracciavano, si baciavano e ballavano le coppie mentre raggio dopo raggio li bagnava con la luce brillante che emanava. Le piaceva il pensiero di avere un ruolo importante nella vita romantica della gente sul grande pianeta Terra.

Da parecchi anni la luna aveva seguito in particolare una coppia che si incontrava ogni mese sulla sponda del Lago Maggiore. Ogni mese sentiva la voce profonda dell'uomo proclamare che lei era l'amore più grande della sua vita e ogni mese vedeva la pelle della donna diventare raggiante in risposta alla sua dichiarazione. E la luna brillava più forte, godendo all'idea che fosse lei a rafforzare il loro amore.

Una notte scura come un bulbo di giacinto, un brutto spettacolo si presentò alla sua vista e per la prima volta della sua esistenza la luna divenne pallida. Quella notte l'uomo non si incontrò con "l'amore più grande della sua vita" ma con un' altra. La luna si sentì così male e triste che non riusciva più a guardare. Questo tradimento significava per lei la fine della sua fiducia nell'amore sulla pianeta Terra e quella notte la luce brillante della luna si spense.

I Capelli di Clara

La caracteristica più attraente di Clara erano i suoi capelli lunghi, lunghi. Li ha lasciati crescere quando era incinta, sapendo che la crescita aumenta durante una gravidanza per causa degli ormoni. Io ero contro: non ero attratto dal tipo di donna coi capelli lunghi.

Quando il nostro bimbo aveva 4 anni, i capelli di Clara avevano una lunghezza di circa un mezzo metro. Li portava spesso sciolti e anche se lo tenevo sempre nascosto, mia moglie mi piaceva moltissimo così. Non so il perché, ma non me la sentivo di dirglielo. Forse sono un uomo testardo e poco romantico.

Tornai a casa dopo una giornata all' impresa straordinariamente stancante. Come sempre, Clara mi salutò con un abbraccio. All' improvviso mi sentii malissimo: un insieme di collera e rimpianto assalivano il mio cuore e mi riempivano di autocommiserazione e aversione per mia moglie.

"Cosa diavolo hai fatto?" gridai.

"Mi sono fatta tagliare i capelli," rispose lei, ridendo.

"Ma non mi hai chiesto il permesso!" ribattei.

"Permesso? Per che cosa? Per andare dal parrucchiere?" chiese Clara, gli occhi spalancati come una chi non ci capisce più niente.

"Ma sì! Non mi hai nemmeno informato!"

"Non sapevo che ci tenessi molto di miei capelli lunghi!"

"Già. Moltissimo."

"Spiace. Oggi ero in piscina e mi sono accorta che non ci vado spesso perché è sempre un lavoraccio coi capelli. Quindi sono andata subito dopo dal parrucchiere. Se tu avessi detto qualcosa non li avrei lasciati tagliare così corti!"

La Nostra Pendola

Da un'eternità l'albero cresce sul pianeta e rappresenta per me una sorta di pendola che segna per l'intero universo il tempo. I suoi rami sono come delle lancette che indicano le ore del giorno, il suo fogliame è come un' orologeria naturale che ticchetta il passo delle stagioni, la sua corteccia è come un pendolo gigante sulla quale si vedono mille tracce e segni del passare degli anni.

Oscillando al ritmo dei venti, battendo in sintonia con le piogge, suonando al tuono delle tempeste, contando il movimento del sole e della luna, l'albero spunta, cresce e scambia i colori in armonia con la natura. E ogni anno la natura gli regala un cerchio che serve come testimonianza della sua crescità.

Con le radici è vicino al cuore della Terra più di qualunque altra cosa e con la sua chioma è il più vicino al cielo. Sulla Terra da 370 milioni di anni, l'albero ebbe tanto tempo da risucchiare molta sapienza e molta saggezza. Fermo nello stesso posto per l'intera durata della sua vita, sorveglia silenziosamente ogni sviluppo, ogni cambiamento, ogni sbaglio e ogni successo che si svolge sul pianeta.

Un giorno, l'uomo non si accontentò del metodo che offriva la natura per contare il tempo e inventò l'orologio meccanico. Divide il giorno in ore; le ore in minuti; i minuti in secondi e si constringe a seguire un ritmo artificiale. Giorno per giorno, si preoccupa di ogni secondo perso, di ogni minuto di ritardo, di ogni ora sprecata, ma non abbastanza di milioni di alberi tagliati, ammalati o morti.

L' Esame

Nonostante la sua riluttanza l'alunno entrò nell' aula della scuola per dare l'esame di matematica. Ignorando la trepidazione che sentiva, si spostò in avanti con passi grandi per dare l'impressione che fosse sicuro di sé. Mentre prendeva le prove d'esame dalle mani scarne dell' insegnante, commise l'errore di guardarlo in faccia: dal suo volto traspariva un crudele cinismo. Non potendo evitarlo, i pensieri negativi che emanava l' insegnante invasero la sua anima.

Disorientato, l'alunno comminciò a scrivere...

Tre ore più tardi, si spostò in avanti con passi piccoli, esitò, poi disse: 'Eccolo qua – l'esame. Sono bocciato come l'ha voluto Lei dall' inizio!' E gettò i suoi fogli a terra.

Anni dopo si sussurava che questo alunno fosse stato Albert Einstein. L'insegnante che ignorò il suo talento in matematica aveva sempre cancellato tutte le sue theorie 'strane' che tendeva a scrivere sul quaderno, dicendo che erano 'idiozie scritte da un allievo stupido.'

La Studentessa

"Figurati che ho appena visto la nostra amica Carolina in biblioteca – stava leggendo un libro e scrivendo appunti. Quando sono uscita, il suo foglio era già gremito di scrittura."

"Come mai? Ognuno di noi sa che a lei non piace leggere – tanto meno scrivere la sua impressione di un libro!"

"Lo so - si trattienne a stento di leggere quello che è scritto sulla copertina, poi guarda sul internet per vedere se esiste una recensione del libro. Se ce n'è, non esita a estrarre il più possiblile dal testo, stamparlo, e consegnarlo al docente come se fosse lavoro suo. In realtà lei non ha mai interpretato una opera litteraria. Io non capisco perchè ha scelto la Letteratura, neanche come è riuscita ad essere accettato per il corso."

In questo momento la ragazza, già uscita dalla biblioteca è ascoltando da un tempo i pettegolezzi delle sue amiche, dice:

"Voi non avete mai letto 'Seta' di Alessandro Baricco, guisto? Per questo non potrete capire il perchè!"

E con vaga insofferenza continua:

"Stavo cercando il libro perfetto: una scrittura semplice, leggera, impercettibile... una storia seducente, silenziosa e piena di tenerezza. Adesso l'ho trovato. Ecco perchè!"

Il Vecchio Libro

Mentre svuotavo un antico arredo che per tanti anni si trovava nella soffitta della casa dei miei genitori, scovai un vecchissimo libro. Non era possibile leggere né il titolo, né il nome dell' autore tanto era danneggiato il frontespizio. Subito mi ricordai le parole di Papà: aveva sempre retenuto che prima di sposarsi con lui, Mamma avesse butato via una collezione di libri che secondo lui avrebbe potuto avere un valore inestimabile. Mamma li aveva comprati da bambina al mercatino dei libri usati che la biblioteca nazionale di Londra teneva ogni anno. Anni dopo si veniva a sapere che un rarissimo libro firmato dall' autore Bram Stoker nel 1897 era sparito dell' archivio della biblioteca proprio il giorno in cui c'era stato il mercatino. Correva voce che fu erroneamente venduto, ma l' appello al publico per ritrovarlo non rendeva nessun resultato.

Lo presi dal posto nascosto e lo misi con cura sul tavolo in salotto per meglio esaminare il contenuto. L'aprii. La carta era gialla e friabile. Non potevo vedere nessuna scrittura – le pagine sembravano vuote. Improvvisamente il libro mi sfuggii di mano, cadde a terra e si sbriciolò. Fra i pezzetti di carta c'era una foto – in nero seppia. Riconobbi Mamma. Riconobbi il personnaggio seduto accanto a lei: Il Conte Dracula – i denti lunghi e affilati già dentro il suo collo. Gridai e corsi fuori dalla casa.

Quando fui più calma, telefonai a mio fratello. Mi raccontò che conosceva la foto. Era stata l'idea di Papà di travestirsi da vampiro e farsi fotografare con la mamma. 'Era solo un scherzo,' dice e ride per il mio terrore.

Una Nascità Rapida

Un martedì in Inghilterra -
nel cuore della primavera
decisi di andarmene
dall' utero di 'Mummy'.
Era notte - lo sapevo già -
sentii il russare; il canto di papà.
Mamma - essendo esperta di parto
andò in bagno e aprì il rubinetto.
I precedenti erano stati lunghi -
uno dieci ore, l'altro due giorni
'Tempo ce n'è,' disse mia madre
'E l'acqua calda ha un effetto calmante.'
Appena immerso il suo corpo
fu inondata da un dolore acuto
e non potendo resistere
cominciò con forza a spingere -
ed a gridare – voce piena d'urgenza
'Per favore chiama l'ostetrica!'
Quando papà entrò in bagno
dove lei stava partorendo
era già visibile il mio cranio
e mio padre in preda al panico
le comandò 'blocca il parto!'
e 'per favore aspetta il medico!'
Ma caspita - non fu possibile –
Il processo di nascita è inarrestabile!

Non seguendo il suo consiglio
continuava a partorire il figlio.
E mentre lui telefonava
sentiva lei che urlava:

'Puoi dire al gentile dottore
che è arrivata in meno di due ore
velocissima, ma sana e bella
per le nostre bambine, una sorella!'
Dopodichè, stanca e sconvolta
di una nascita veramente insolita
alle tre del mattino quel martedì,
mia mamma svenne, poi dormì.

Danza Settimanale

Non ti parlo,
ma una volta la settimana,
ti vedo nello studio di danza
e balliamo insieme davanti allo specchio.

Mi piace la tua spontaneità.
Mi piace la tua energia.
Mi fa piacere vederti
così
vivace.

Ogni martedì ti vedo
sempre piena di gioia,
sempre te stessa
e comunque -

Ti detesto!
Quando ti vedo, vedo anche
la mia stanchezza,
la mia manchevolezza,
la mia affettazione.

Tu mi mostri che
la mia energia
la mia gioia
la mia spontaneità
sono divenute soltanto riflessi
di te. Comunque -

Ti invito a venire
fuori dallo specchio
a farmi vedere
che anche io sono
come te -
così vivace.

Leone sul Divano

Che re degli animali!
Con la tua criniera anodata,
le tue gambe penzoloni,
le tue zampe morbide.

Ho chiesto un sogno e eccoti qua!
Che cosa vuoi dirmi?
Che sono debole?
Che sono stanca?
Che mi mancano
il corragio
la forza?

Hai ragione, tu -
eccomi qua, l'artista molle:
niente sangue,
niente ossa,
niente stomaco -
un corpo flaccido e vuoto.

Sono sdraita sul divano
aspettando
un giorno verrà una bimba,
mi terrà tra le braccia,
mi farà le coccole.

LETTERS AND POSTCARDS

Dear writer friend,

I am writing to tell you that writing is the only art you will ever be truly dedicated to and it is the right path for you to take through life.

Writing helps you understand where you are, who you are and opens doors to deep places inside your heart and soul. You need not care or ask what you are writing about, where it is leading or what purpose it serves. These are questions too difficult to answer - besides, no explanation would satisfy your inner cynic who tries time and again to sabotage your writing.

When you write, you are alive. It's as simple as that. Nothing else will give you that unbeatable sensation.

Writing is your witness, proving that you are truly living as it leaves tangible traces on paper. You are somewhat like Clara in Isabel Allende's 'The House of Spirits' - you feel a need to write. Unlike Clara, however, you are not documenting what is happening in the outside world, but you are writing what comes up from the inside. It does not really matter what you actually write about, just engaging in the process of writing is what is important. It will put you into a state of pure connectedness; the inkpot is inside you and you can dip your pen into it and draw from a source of life that links us all, in all our aspects. Through writing, you will find the marriage between the often repetitive and unspectacular and ordinary life on the outside, and the larger, mysterious, profound life on the inside.

Pen and ink are your tools, the act of moving the pen across the page is what affords you access to the source and, in this way, the act of writing is your guide. Your brain and intellect are present but not in charge. Words simply come up through the pen and land on the page, proving to you time and again that you are an instrument in the art - a person willing to co-operate and draw words from the source inside; a source of never-ending ink, forever full and ready to fill page after page.

Writing will carry you through life sanely, sometimes serenely and with grace. Other times, it will whisk you up, throw you down, scream at you with fervour, causing you pain. Do not flee anymore! I know that this is a pain you can welcome - like labour pains in childbirth. The outcome will be new life.

No matter where you are or what is otherwise going on in your life, writing will serve as either anchor, point of reference or lighthouse, depending on what kind of guidance you need. Worries, everyday dramas and niggles, as well as the larger questions and puzzles which sometimes haunt you, can be worked with or become more pliable through writing.

Writing will take you to what's important, show you what needs attention, bring you awareness, insight and occasionally, wisdom. You need not worry about the writing ever leaving you. It will always be there. You don't even need paper or writing pen. You can write thoughts in the air, in the earth, in the water. I have heard stories of prisoners who have written entire novels in their heads, of poets who have memorised all their poems for fear of being persecuted for writing them down. You are lucky in the sense that you live in an age and part of the world in which you are free to express yourself in writing on just about any subject.

I know you are spurned on by a relentless fascination with all that is hidden from sight inside us - our vast, mostly unchartered realm of the unconscious. Your writing will be considered safe by the outside world because you are writing about the inside and most people do not think this is relevant to them or has consequences for the outer world of politics, economics, religion and law, to which more importance is given.

When you write down what comes up from the inner world - your own personal inner world - then that of the collective will come through. In this way, you will be writing about man's soul life, his creative life - not the theory of how it could or should be. It won't be an analysis or explanation but an account of life inside - evidence of which comes up from your source or creative core and lands on paper.

Our modern world tends to favour squeezing out this aspect of our humanness - just like it is squeezing out nature, many of her animals and plants. There is already hardly any space for the creative life in our modern society of fast and hard competition, time pressures and, above all, the need to earn plenty of money. Outside, most decisions are motivated by money and politics. I don't need to tell you this really because I know you know it, but I'd like to think that someone else will pick up this letter one day and read it and so I will repeat myself: the importance and power of money is a man-made illusion we have all become addicted to. It is the concept which has taken us away from living creatively. Everything is measured against money and our creativity cannot be given a price tag. In creative living, we are in heaven where money does not matter, where our souls sing loudly and strongly and individually. In creative living, life is about being in balance, harmony and peace with our inner nature and the nature around us.

We need to re-learn to sit down and doodle in the sand, throw our heads back and enjoy the sensation of raindrops falling on our lips, run through open fields and feel wind ruffling our hair and whistling through our ears. We need to become playful and play - for no reason - no monetary gain, no recognition, no fame. Just play - for the good of the human heart and soul. These 'frivolous' pastimes which are often referred to as indulgent, decadent, childish, irresponsible and only for the lazy or simple, will fill our human hearts with joy. Filling hearts with joy not only has a positive effect on our immediate surroundings but can change the world A joy account when full is just like a healthy bank account - we are rich, we have abundance and have surplus to spend.

Yet we are taught that it is wrong to dream all day, to dance all day, to sing all day or watch the clouds all day. We praise and reward those who sit at a computer all day, watching figures go up and down, getting back ache, high cholesterol and stiff muscles not to mention bad eyesight, irritability, dulling of the creative mind and senses. If you can earn money and can support a family with an activity, it is validated and stamped with society's approval. If it merely fills the heart with joy, makes you feel better balanced and healthy, it is no good.

So, this is why I believe it is imperative that you continue to turn inward and write what you see. Please carry on drawing bucket after bucket from your inner well. This is the source. Eventually, you will draw up answers.

All the best and much courage to you.

From your faithful fellow writing friend,

Penelope Pen xxx

Dear soul sister,

This is Penelope Pen writing to you about a year after my first letter to you. I felt it necessary to put some of my thoughts down in writing and send them to you because I have heard that you are struggling to see clarity and are consequently feeling full of doubt with regard to your writing. Being a writer myself, and your best friend to boot, I am writing in faith and trust that you will want to listen and consider my thoughts on this matter, perhaps even reap some help and advice.

      You really want to get back to regular writing you say, re-open some work you started a number of years ago, but you lack motivation and conviction. First of all, let me remind you that writing is a very important part of your life. As I wrote in my first letter to you: "You are writing <u>for</u> your life" and "nothing else will give you that unbeatable sensation of being part of life; of feeling the pulse of the earth drumming in your heart." Remember those words? This is important because you are a stage in life where there are many other distractions which can lead you away from writing. You need to give writing highest priority and attention. Though you may not know where the writing is leading, whether it will be read or published or have any impact on the outside world at all, please do not forget that it is the effect it has on you that counts the most. Write and you will be healthy and capable of making the necessary steps to go out with the work when the time comes. This is easily said, I know. Practicing it is not easy. A writer without a contract, project, agent, work schedule, pay etc. has great freedom. But you also have a little snag called 'choice'. You can choose to write or not and the outside world will not care. And so, in this situation, you are up against the most powerful and harsh boss of all – Yourself!

      For the past two years, you have been concentrating on settling into a new country... this has involved learning the language, finding your way around geographically, and also administratively and culturally, offering emotional support and guidance to your teenage boys and husband, and acquiring a new house for you all to set up home. These activities have taken up much energy, have given you much cause for anxiety and worry, but have also been a source of joy, excitement and inspiration. You have grown in experience, flexibility, wisdom and are more open to change. These are gifts which will help you grow even more. Recently, you have been feeling a build-up of immense tension. Now that the excitement of the move and the chores of packing and unpacking are over, there's time for you to get back to some of your writing projects. I don't think I am wrong in saying that you have been surprised by how hard you are finding it, how many excuses you come up with, how overwhelmed you feel faced with questions such as: how do I justify the time? What to do with my work once it's finished? This leads you back full circle to the question: what is the point and why write when there are so many other things that need to be done. And because you are familiar with these tormenting questions, you get annoyed and frustrated with yourself that you have not moved on one centimetre since your last writing block.

Oops. I've named it now. Better that way. It's simply a common or garden BLOCK. Everyone has them, repeatedly during a lifetime and probably all the more often if they are artists. So, put the block on the windowsill facing the outside so it can enjoy the view whilst you get on with your important life's work that is *WRITING*.

With warmest wishes for your continued writer's journey.
Your friend and fan club president.

Penelope Pen xxx

Dear creative friend,

It's Penelope Pen writing to you again – this time I not only wish to encourage you in your writing projects, as I have in my past letters, but also in all your other creative endeavours.

I have heard you are in a very creative phase in your life which is wonderful. Congratulations for re-kindling your creative passion and getting back into the flow. Over the years of our friendship, I have witnessed time and again your exceptionally large creative fire and I have also witnessed that keeping this fire burning brightly both inside yourself and in the outside world (without you yourself catching fire and being burned to a frazzle) is not an easy task. I know you have been feeling the precariousness of your situation and so I am writing to you (as your most enthusiastic fan) with the intention of giving you some motivation and moral support.

Being in charge of such a creative fire as yours can put you in a very perilous position; it would not be too dramatic to say that it may sometimes feel as if you are poised between life and death. This is because you need to enter the fire in order to feel the full force and heat of it (as this is your creative source) and yet, you must always do so fully aware of the danger involved and with the strength of mind to find the fire exit for you to escape if necessary. You are forced to live your creative life, therefore, in a position of extreme tension between you the fragile, vulnerable human being and you, the powerful creative spirit (that can also quite easily become an almighty destructive spirit).

Not only do you have to contend with your creative force within, but also with your need to be a normal human being outside in the everyday, real world. This creates other areas of conflict:

❖ There is a drive in you to shine and be exceptional and unique in all you do. Yet you also harbour a desire to be small and live a

339

quiet, insignificant existence in a community in which you can relax and feel you are accepted and loved as one of a group.

❖ You dream of great heights, recognition for your talents, fame for your achievements (and possibly, fortune); yet you are both afraid of success and afraid of failure and this often keeps you in a stall position; you neither advance, nor step back but secretly wait for the world to finally discover you.

❖ You know you have great gifts and that it is your duty and birth right to make the best use of them. Yet, every time you flaunt them, you feel such guilt and shame that you soon retract and make yourself silent again.

First of all, let me assure you that you are not the first person to come up against these kinds of strong conflicts – I'm afraid it is the fate of a highly creative person to also be incredibly introverted and painfully sensitive. In your case, you have also been given a good-sized dollop of guilt on top of your creative mountain. This 'cream topping' makes you feel unworthy of your gifts and shame for expressing them.

I think you know yourself that one of the most important keys to overcoming these conflicts is acceptance:

❖ Acceptance that you are sensitive, introverted and often very shy.
❖ Acceptance that you cannot change the way you have been made.
❖ Acceptance that this is your destiny.

It helps if you understand why you struggle in some situations more than others and it also helps to know that there are some choices you can make to ease certain conflicts. In this way, you can influence the direction in which your artist goes – i.e. towards the creative rather than towards the destructive.

As you already know (because you have done the deep work necessary to have this wisdom), the way we react or behave is sometimes dictated or triggered by certain childhood dramas. The hurt child inside you will always want to be small and go un-noticed because that was your role in the family. You spent a great deal of your childhood holding yourself back, being afraid to shine too brightly in case you spoiled it for others (especially your sisters). The consequence was that you went underground with your need to create: you did it secretly, alone, quietly, timidly, for yourself. You didn't realise how talented you were or how much other people could benefit from seeing your work, or how honourable sharing can actually be. The work you showed never earned your artist recognition in the world at large. You received a very low grade for your 'A' level art; you were discouraged from following an artist's life by your teachers, preferring you to study something more worthwhile. In your childhood home, there was place for one artist only and that was the first born. The message to you was that, under no circumstances were you to venture on that territory because it was not yours.

You yearn to feel part of groups, yet mostly you feel you are an outsider, a misfit, a foreign body and that people in the group dislike you and will reject you if you are not careful what you say, do, or how you act. If they see what talents you have, you say to yourself, then they really will reject me... and so you keep that part quiet, maybe giving a little bit away, but you do not hint at the massiveness of your creativity. I think this is partly because of your childhood experience of keeping yourself small inside the family unit, but also partly because you are still unprepared and lack the confidence to take on the full responsibility for your large dollop of creative talent. 'People will expect great things from me and I am afraid I will disappoint them and they will find out I am actually only a normal, weak human being with nothing really important to say or contribute to the world we live in.' Sound familiar?

Feeling this way: vulnerability, fragility, pain, distress at your limited humanness – these are also gifts because without them, you would not have access to that abundance of exceptional, diverse, soul-felt creativity.

Just remember that when the time comes for you to stride out into the world and show who you really are, what you are really capable of, and just how strongly you believe in creativity as the way forward for all of mankind, you not only have Penelope Pen at your side, but you also have the confidence and strength inside. You can stand tall and shine. You can. I believe in you.

So, take heart and hug yourself today from me and please do not forget how far you have already come.

You can live the creative life and you will one day be seen in the world. You need not be loud about it, or run around trying to get attention; it will come automatically to you. You just need to believe in yourself as artist, continue with the work and try to be as authentic as possible.

With much love, and belief in you,

Penelope Pen xxx

My dear friend,

Thank you for your letter. My goodness, so much has happened since I last wrote to you nine months ago. Your first-born has been living his independent life-adventure in the United Kingdom for almost five months. You write that you have missed his company, the many little chats you used to have during the week – 'snippets' of his life that made you feel so much a part of it. I can imagine how hard it must be to let go of the first child, but it sounds like you have done a pretty good job; allowing him to stand on his own feet, make his own mistakes and learn from them, without interfering or trying to rescue him. That, my dear friend is the greatest gift a mother can give. Don't forget that! That inner judge of yours can be so vicious at times. Well, all I can say is: Don't believe a word he says! It's all lies with a capital L. He just does it because he can get you all worked up and spin you into a depression.

      Sounds like you didn't just enter a depression, but a full-bodied dark night of the soul. The way you describe it gives me the chills.

"An awful dark place from which there seems to be no return, no matter how hard you search for a way out. And all the good you ever did in the world, your positive beliefs about yourself, any foundations you thought you had, are no longer there. Beneath you is a void – nothing to catch you or support you or help you. Most frightening of all is the lack of light. There is only judgment and you have been damned to suffer a life of failure, guilt, shame and fear. The only way out is to feel those soul-destroying emotions until they penetrate to your core. Yet you must not let them consume you, lest you be dragged down into the depths of eternal darkness and be lost forever."

      I take my hat off to you for getting out of that one. Why didn't you call on my help sooner? You needn't answer that question.

When you are in such a dark place, it is near to impossible to reach out for help from someone and probably just as impossible for that someone to help anyway. I am all the happier to hear that you made it out the other end and are gradually regaining strength and confidence. But don't be surprised if you continue to feel fragile for a while longer, you're bound to after that experience.

You say that your morning writing practice has helped you get out of that terrible dark place and that their power is magical. I cannot agree with you more. So, on that note, I shall sign off with the words: Write, write, write...

Much love from Penelope, your faithful friend and admirer xxx

Dearest soul sister,

It's been over a year since you last contacted me and I was just wondering how you were getting on, when I heard your call for some support. You say you are in quite a quandary as to how to shape or 'create' the next phase in your life. You are very much aware that your youngest son will be leaving home in the near future and look forward to more freedom as far as any personal choices are concerned; yet you are also aware how hard it will be for you to say goodbye to him and to your role of stay-at-home mum. It sounds like you are excited about the prospect of exploring other interests and possibly embarking on projects or finding paid work and at the same time, somewhat apprehensive, scared even, by this kind of freedom.

Whilst pondering over how to start this letter to you this morning, I had a flash of insight and then, all of a sudden, I saw the image of a swan. Remember how as a child, your favourite fairy tale was "The Ugly Duckling"? When you began Jungian Analysis and were introduced to the idea that fairy tales often reveal your personal story or drama of childhood, you realised in an instant that as a child, you had truly felt just like the ugly duckling had in his family of ducks - alone, out of place, sad, miserable, and ultimately, rejected. You also discovered that as an adult, the poor, sad, ugly duckling was still inside you and was the reason why you kept on re-living those upsetting emotions of loneliness and rejection over and over again. I can imagine that moving and settling in Italy will have brought with it many ugly duckling moments!

So, I thought I would remind you that "The Ugly Duckling" is a tale about personal transformation for the better.

Remember when the ugly duckling sees the swans flying overhead and gets so excited by the sight of such magnificent creatures, that he immediately wants to fly up to them and take a closer look – but, alas, he can't fly. Rejected by ducks, hens, other

345

farmyard animals and children, he wanders off and spends a cold, miserable winter all alone. When spring arrives and he sees the wild swans landing on a lake in front of him, he decides to come out of hiding and literally offer himself to them as a kind of sacrifice: he'd rather be killed by such beautiful birds than continue a life of misery. And that's when he discovers the miracle: he is a swan himself. He opens his wide white wings and takes flight, soaring to happiness and freedom with his new family.

I think that you have known for a long time that there is a swan inside you, too, yet have continued to identify with the ugly duckling. It sounds strange, but this is often what happens: you live your life as something you are not, just because it's what you are most familiar with. My hunch is that you have kind of grown attached to feeling you don't belong, and live with rejection and loneliness as if they were your life forces. Well, my dear, wonderful friend - It's time to discover your swan wings and go fly with them.

How? I hear you ask. Time and patience. The Ugly Duckling didn't have any tasks to do. No slaying of dragons or passing ogre's tests; no dangerous journeys to places to find a special object, or magic potion. He simply had to sit out the cold winter without knowing what was in store for him, all the time suspecting the worst. But then in the spring, hey presto! There he stood - a magnificent swan!

This is the way for you, too. Yours is a time of patient waiting. Accept that striving to force things or running around seeking answers is not the way. By all means continue the yoga practice, keep on writing the pages, meditate, muse, philosophise - these will help you thorough this period of waiting. If you can accept that all is right just as it is, that you need not change a thing, you will not drive yourself crazy with restlessness in the realm of not knowing.

Your soul sister and writer friend,
Penelope Pen xxx

Hello my dear, dear friend,

How lovely it was to read your recent letter. It was brimming with so much energy and enthusiasm for your future plans that I felt my heart's voice singing in tune with it, too. Thank you - it was a wonderful experience.

Your excitement at the idea of embarking on the MA course with the Open University showed how much it was resonating loudly and clearly within you: you had finally found a project into which you could pour the knowledge and experience you had acquired over the years; you could build on your formal education and you would have a structure to support research into many exciting revolutionary projects in the fields of education and creativity. Not only were you looking forward to a structured programme for the coming years, but also to receiving recognition and encouragement along the way. Suddenly you had discovered some direction and purpose to the post-children era. You were convinced that you had found a stimulating path that would not only give your intellect a boost, but would challenge you to expand your skills and push yourself to a higher level of professionalism and attainment.

The dream you had about 10 years ago of a School of Creativity came gushing back. It all made sense. Being the Year of the Dragon gave you even more of a boost and convinced you of the 'rightness' of the decision to embark on the Masters degree. Doors opened in your mind's eye - ones to a new role as inventor or facilitator of a school of the future - one in which Creativity, Mindfulness, Multilingualism and Self-Exploration play key roles. You saw yourself working again, perhaps finding a role at the International School of Milan. Sir Ken Robinson further reinforced these ideas that this was definitely the direction you'd like to take and his TED speeches were like nectar to your thirsty creative mind.

Then, today, another letter arrived. What a contrast! No more creative juices or sparks of delight; just disappointment and grief. You lamented that you had 'fallen off the new-found structured path to the future and back into the darkness and chaos of the unknown.'

Now that I have read and re-read your letter a couple of times, I can confidently reply: better that way. You are free again. You are no longer running the risk of becoming trapped by conformity, stuffy intellectual discussions and the need to be patted on the head by established institutions. Before I explain, I would first like to say how brave it was of you to not only look critically at the course content and your reasons for embarking on it, but also to have the courage to pull your own emergency brakes.

After having had time to look at the set books for the course myself, I fully agree with you: a Master's degree in Education with specialisation in Applied Linguistics would have entailed wading through many dry seas of intellectual material that would have had the potential to kill your creativity and passion altogether. Ok, so you were attracted by the idea of achieving something that would give you recognition and social status. There's nothing wrong with that, but there are other paths you can take and I have no doubt in my mind that they will reveal themselves to you in due course. Your creative bell has rung and now all kinds of synchronicities and intuitive 'calls' will ensue. Recognising that the Open University direction was a bark up the wrong tree is a good thing.

That quest was probably being led by the young career woman inside you who thrives on conformity and attainment. I bet she got so very excited because she thought she was about to get the starring role in your second half of life. Well, it's a blow to her that this is not going to be the case, but a great step forward for you, the essential you. As you say yourself, the one more suited to leading you into the next stage of your life is the silent, quiet, conscientious one who sits at the back of the class and who has hardly said a word all year.

Diana, my hunch is that she's the swan. Remember? She is waiting patiently for her white wings to develop and mature. In the spring, the air will lift her to the skies with effortless grace and she'll fly to heights unimaginable in the vast, limitless blue sky.

I have full and absolute faith in your ability to find your way and I believe you will be in your element before the year is out. Before I sign off, I would like to remind you of your idea to put together your own, personalised education programme. I quote: I'm planning to also do a kind of gap year and am looking at putting together my own training course by signing up for various workshops / conferences / courses with teachers I connect with and who are involved in areas that interest me (Psychology, Spirituality, Mindfulness, Body work and Dream work).

Wishing you the very best of luck in that venture.

Love from Penelope Pen xxx

Postcard I

Dearest,

I was wondering why you had been so silent...and then this morning I received your postcard asking for directions to 'Heaven on Earth'.

Keep on travelling until you get to Flow. At the first junction, follow the signs to Heart, past Nowhere-in-Particular, on to Non-Judgement and Surrender. You should then be able to see the horizon. Keep on going until Anywhere. This road is very long and has many bends and forks. Just keep heading in the direction that feels right.

When you have given up all expectations of ever arriving, you will be getting close.

I hope you make it. It is peaceful here and you get to paint and write all day without feeling guilty. Furthermore, time stands still, so you never ever waste yours or anyone else's time, no matter what you do or don't do.

Best of luck,
Love P xxx

Postcard II

My dear friend,

In your last postcard, you wondered whether you had a
sanctuary for your creative projects. You do indeed
have such a place!

Your sanctuary is a small house in the garden, separate
to the house in which you live with your family. In
that house, you can breathe the creative air, feel the
creative fire and answer the creative call. In that
house, there are no domestic chores, no children to look
after, husbands or others to please. Troubles and
problems of everyday are far away and complexities of
life, love and marriage do not exist.

There inside your small house in the garden, creating is
the point of everything and there is no need to do or
say anything to prove, justify or manifest your
existence.

You simply are. You live. You are alive.
And <u>that</u> is enough.
Xx P

Postcard III

Dear soul sister,

I am writing to you to say: just write! Don't worry about publishers for now or it'll prevent you from working. Just do your work and all else will reveal itself when the time comes. Have faith in the greater plan. It's not necessary to run around shaking trees now. You may get the fruit fall you wish for or they may all tumble and bury you alive!
All the best,
xx P

Dear Pen (elope),

I am writing to tell you about an epiphanic experience I had. It was as if the penny had finally dropped (excuse the pun!). As if being struck by lightning in a corny cartoon, I suddenly felt the essence of who I am. It seemed ridiculously simple, but true: I was just there, alive, present. I felt as if a very real and vast container was sustaining my life as well as everyone else's. Everything made sense. It felt like a miracle. The search was over: I finally got it! There is no need to search. There is no answer. There is possibly not even a question.

All around us is mystery and unknowing and everything we can and cannot possibly imagine or grasp. Yet, we are part of it – and the only thing we need to do during our life here on Earth is participate. There's no need to grab, question, hold on, control, channel, understand. We need not describe it, manipulate it, sell it, package it, or teach it... All there is to do is listen. Everything else will just happen, if we let it. That is the essence of life. All the rest: superficial pass-times and distractions.

I am no longer in a hurry to get somewhere; I am ready to let it come to me. All the while, I will do my best to meet life as a human on planet Earth, with grace, humility and integrity.

I am whole and always have been. The cracks and wounds are to the personality and to the ego and the part of me that thinks it is separate from God. I am not separate. I am a part of the whole. I am whole.

This brings me great hope and joy that one day there will be the leap in consciousness necessary to ease us all into the knowing that there is no need to run around fighting, blaming, squabbling, competing, killing.

It matters what I do in this present moment and that I am present for it. If I can manage that over and again, this will be the grace you have talked about.

In deep gratitude to you dear Pen,

Love from Diana xxx

Postcard IV

Dear Creative,

My name is Lu Sun Ming Tang and I bow down to you. I do not know you or ask you if you are worthy of my bow. I know you are.

I wear a straw hat to protect my bald head and to give me a friendlier, more human look. Though I am small and silent, I am solid, made of sacred stone which has been carefully carved over millennia.

I am unbreakable and untouchable, yet forever present and guarding that which is most sacred within. I am sending you this postcard because you called me through your dreams.

I say this: within you is a spirit child that must be invisible for the moment, guarded and kept safe, but will be there when the time comes for you to dance the child's dance, sing the child's song and speak the child's tale. She is small. She is patient. She is very, very strong.

AFTERWORD AND RESOURCES

About the Author: Spiritual Autobiography

I was christened by my parents: father, British from the Church of England; mother, German and Catholic, but neither practicing. There was the odd visit to the church near to where I lived in the UK until the age of 7, but other than that, I received sparse religious or spiritual guidance from my parents, from the church or from my school. I didn't feel I was missing out, or curious to know more about religion.

I presumed that I didn't believe in God; that I didn't believe in anything much and that it wasn't important anyway. It wasn't until much later (my late thirties) that I asked myself whether I might indeed believe in either a God, or something that could be considered spiritual or greater than what I considered to be me, myself, I.

When I was 18, I had a boyfriend who asked me one day about my thoughts on God. I told him that I had none. He couldn't understand my disinterest and admitted openly and passionately to me that if he didn't believe in God he would die. I couldn't relate to that at all. It puzzled me and stayed with me.

In my early twenties at a social gathering with my sister's friends, I became quite notorious for spontaneously exclaiming: "I just don't know who I am!" Everyone who was standing around me at the time found this amusing (including me); yet I recognized that my sudden outburst had come from a deep place of yearning.

My life tootled along. I got married to a German, moved to Luxembourg and had 2 children. I enjoyed being a mum, wife and work colleague, embracing it all until it all apparently became too much and I became 'unstuck'. This was around the age of 34.

I had suddenly become aware of a loud voice inside my head that had strong negative opinions and judgements about who I was. The voice was relentless, continued day and night and became louder and louder, especially if I tried to ignore it. It would go on and on, screaming all the reasons why I was not good enough, a nothing, a no one and how I was worthless, fit only for the rubbish bin. It didn't take long before I derailed, having what my doctor called 'burnout'. Thankfully, I was given a month off work, did not accept medication from the psychiatrist, but used this time to recover and reflect.

Though I didn't realise it at the time, this was the beginning of my very serious and committed spiritual path and search to find some answers to that fundamental question: who am I?

My first instinct was to help myself somehow and I did this by reaching for a book called 'The Artist's Way' by Julia Cameron. I had been given that book by my dear friend Sarah a few years earlier, yet had cast it aside, annoyed that it involved doing certain exercises I didn't feel ready for. In this moment of burnout, however, it was the best thing that could have come into my life.

The Artist's Way is a twelve-week self-help course in "uncovering and re-discovering your creative self". I followed it religiously, completing all the exercises and using the main tools: Morning Pages, 3 pages of stream-of-consciousness writing each morning; and The Artist's Date – a date with yourself to do whatever you like once per week. The course introduced me to a felt sense of a Great Creator and introduced me to the concept of synchronicity, or meaningful coincidence, which in turn (and quite synchronistically) led me to the discovery of C.G. Jung and Jungian Psychoanalysis.

As luck would have it, I found the only (at that time) Jungian psychoanalyst in Luxembourg (where I was currently living) and I became an analysand for one year. During that year, I dove deeply into the question, who am I, through the meetings with the analyst, the analysis of dreams, universal and personal symbols, and fairytales. It was challenging: at times painful and excruciatingly difficult; at times thrilling and exhilarating. I was uncovering all kinds of truths about who I was and who I was not and it culminated in a book (to date unpublished), entitled 'Lighting Up My House'. The writing of that book was my way of digesting and integrating the work I had done with my analyst over the year.

Circumstances moved me away from Luxembourg in 2005 to Italy. In this new country, I primarily busied myself with learning a new language (Italian) and getting to grips with my new home, environment and culture. And yet, surprisingly, this new home lent itself to continuing my exploration of Jungian Psychology and philosophy. Zurich was not too far away and some seminars were offered in Ascona on Lake Maggiore where I lived. I was able to participate in various workshops and seminars in Switzerland and Italy and deepen my understanding of the Jungian approach.

All the time, in the background, I was working on a book entitled 'Living the Animal'. For me, this book was another spiritual practice, a bit like Lighting Up My House. Writing had become a trustworthy way of embodying the work and the teachings.

In 2013, I travelled to India, discovered yoga and meditation, and began exploring those paths. After my return, I started teaching yoga and had the opportunity to participate in various meditation trainings, including Vipassana Meditation as taught by S.N. Goenka.

My source for reading and teachings during my time in Italy was principally the internet (YouTube, iTunes Podcasts etc.). I discovered the website SoundsTrue.com, founded by Tami Simon and was in heaven! Tami Simon continues to provide a wealth and richness of resources for spiritual awakening.

It was on the Sounds True website and through their dedicated newsletters, that I learned about many diverse teachings and teachers, including Gangaji and Eli. They were offering so-called *Satsang* in Baden-Baden, Germany, not far from where I was living and I signed up for it. *Satsang* is a Sanskrit term meaning "being in the company of the truth" or "right association," and refers to a group of like-minded people who engage in a spiritual dialogue. This was a groundbreaking experience as it showed me how, at the core, we are all the same and have the same yearning to know our true selves.

Further along the road, I came across Tara Brach, her teachings, Radical Self-Acceptance, and her weekly talks, Tara Talks: a web series that she hosts and broadcasts on YouTube. In her work, I discovered a combination of Western psychology and Eastern spiritual practices. She was showing me how to pay mindful attention to my inner life in a loving and compassionate way. Her talks are full of humanness and humour that support people in engaging fully with the world.

Tich Nhat Hanh was another discovery and I was lucky enough to go on a week's retreat to Plum Village in France and 'play' at being a nun. Though I often yearned to stay in retreat and live a life of a monastic, I realised that was not my calling. Another realisation I made was that, regardless of whether you live the monastic life or not, we are all on the same spiritual path. During the time at Plum Village, I had expected the monks and nuns to be completely different to me, much more evolved, spiritual and competent at mindfulness; but my eyes were opened. I met some grumpy, some moody, some jolly, some angry monks, some unhappy, some obedient, some daring and some defiant nuns – simply: other fellow humans who were just doing their best, as I was, to live their lives mindfully and as wholly as possible.

Another teacher I discovered, first through my friend Sarah and then again through Sounds True was Pema Chödrön (who immediately became a favourite mentor of mine - a woman who really does walk her talk).

I felt especially helped and supported in everyday life through her teachings on how to work with *Shenpa* (the urge or hook that triggers our habitual tendency to close down), as well as her no-nonsense, humorous approach to meditation and to being human.

In my heart, I knew I wanted to explore meditation further, perhaps teach it, or at least nurture it in others. This had been inspired by reading and listening to Jon Kabat-Zinn and is what led me to sign up for an 8-week MBSR course (Mindfulness Based Stress Reduction) in Milan. After the MBSR training, it was recommended we attend a silent meditation retreat led by visiting Zen masters Melissa Myozen Blacker, Roshi and David Dae An Rynick, Roshi founders of Boundless Way Zen, Worcester, Massachusetts, USA.

That 5-day meditation retreat left a lasting impression on me. I felt a homecoming there like never before. Not long afterwards, I ordered David's book: This Truth Never Fails, lapped it up and then emailed him with some questions. I didn't know what I wanted from the contact with him, I just knew I needed to contact him. I ended up having life coaching sessions with him over a six-month period. One of the outcomes was the website and blog www.poet-in-residence.net.

It was also at that meditation retreat that I learned about *sesshin,*[30] and that there would be a three-week winter *sesshin* the following January at their Boundless Way Zen Temple in Massachusetts, USA. As soon as I heard this, my heart leapt; the idea of spending three weeks in meditation was what I was yearning for. Even so, there was some hesitation: it would mean travelling a long way and it would mean a month away from home (I was nervous about my husband's reaction to this, not least because I couldn't imagine him being thrilled about it like I was). We talked. He recognised that this was something of great importance to me, something that filled me with joy, and he encouraged me to go. I did.

As on shorter retreats, during this long *sesshin* I re-discovered the power of silence; how it can transport us into a deep heart space; a sacred realm that is fully alive, pulsating with human compassion and connection. Furthermore, I felt an undeniable and tangible sense of community, of belonging to the human family. As I sat there alone on my cushion, with my breath, my thoughts, my body, I felt the togetherness, the beingness 'with' others - fully supported and sustained simply by their presence, by their practice. Touching that, I knew on a deep level we are One, we are all included in the whole multifaceted web of life and as such, we are all an intrinsic part of the whole - the breath within the breath. Whilst at the temple, I decided I would like to deepen my practice and requested guidance from Melissa Myozen Blacker, Roshi. She agreed to be my primary spiritual teacher (*shoken*[31]) with whom I would continue to have formal practice interviews

---

[30] Sesshin can be literally translated as "touching the heart-mind". It is a period of intense meditation in a Zen monastery or temple. In this case, it was held at the Boundless Way Temple, Worcester, Massechussettes. Over a single day, there were repeated times for zazen, kinhin (walking meditation), dokusan (individual meetings with a teacher), teacher talks, and dharma dialogue.

[31] **Shoken:** a primary relationship with one transmitted teacher. This primary teacher-student relationship is traditionally called shoken, which literally means "seeing one another."

(*dokusan*[32]) when I returned home. That agreement was invaluable to me; Melissa helped me settle back home, and find orientation over the post-*sesshin* months whilst I was somewhat confused about the direction I was taking. Though I felt at ease in the Buddhist community and found my teacher and the teachings most relevant and insightful, there was something about this formal relationship and commitment to a Buddhist path that just would not sit well with me. It soon became apparent that I wanted to be free of any formal direction or teaching when it came to spirituality. After several months of *dokusan* meetings, I ended the formal teacher-student relationship and returned to my free-style approach.

I continued learning and studying in that way – committed to the spiritual path of awakening, but not to any one specific religion, prescribed path, or way. I did meditation practice either on my own or in small groups (if I could find people willing to sit); I practiced yoga and wrote my morning pages each day. I discovered over and over again that I had all the support I needed and I needed to walk it my way. One thing was clear – no matter what, I wanted to dedicate my life to it.

It is from that place of yearning for spiritual awakening and dedication to the spiritual path that I began *from Pen (elope) with love xxx.*

I trust that all paths, all religions, all spiritual teachings and teachers, are pointing us in the direction of wholeness, and oneness. There is no right or wrong way to go about spiritual awakening, but I believe it is paramount that we stay true to ourselves.

My true way seems to be a combination of the many teachings I receive from writers, poets, philosophers and other spiritual teachers I read or encounter; my practices of writing, yoga

---

[32] Dokusan: within Boundless Way Zen, committed students are encouraged to attend private meetings with transmitted teachers and senior dharma teachers. These meetings are referred to as dokusan, which in Japanese means going alone to the teacher.

and meditation; and everyday life challenges, experiences and relationships.

What an amazing, bizarre, fascinating and miraculous journey it is!

With deep gratitude to all who travel the spiritual path and, by doing so, support me, and others on our unique journey.

With love,
Diana xxx

Poet in Residence Blog and Press

Poet in Residence is the name of the blog I created five years ago, www.poet-in-residence.net - a space for poets' voices who write in English but who live in different countries. The blog is a way of letting voices be heard that otherwise may not be heard because the work is hidden away on a computer disk, inside a notebook or a desk drawer. It is a way of honouring other poets whether or not they consider themselves 'real' poets, and gives their work a chance to go out into the world and touch another human being.

The idea for the blog initially came from my desire to send my own work out into the world and a frustration that I had no outlet or publisher for it.

When I expressed this frustration to my life coach at the time, he suggested I create a blog. I had no idea what a blog was, let alone how to create one, but when he set it as 'homework', I set about doing it. I soon discovered there was a wealth of online support in the form of videos and other instructional information. I didn't really know what kind of writing I would like to publish on the blog, but then found myself daydreaming about what it might be like to be a poet in residence. And there I had it! I decided to make myself 'Poet in Residence' of my own home and promptly wrote my first poem for the blog, entitled Poet in Residence (see the section Poems for Writers). In that moment, I 'signed' a contract with myself to give writing utmost importance in my life. I also made a promise: to keep an open heart, invite gentleness, compassion and, above-all, non-judgment to be with me as I put pen to paper (or, fingertips to keyboard). Please feel free to visit the website and enjoy the many voices found there.

Another daydream of mine is to set up my own publishing company. Though this is not yet the case, this first publication is a step in that direction and this is the logo I have created.

Teachings and Wise Words Along the Way

Over the years, I have benefitted from many wise teachings in many forms, such as books, courses, workshops and retreats; diverse online offerings such as videos, events and podcasts; as well as many invaluable conversations, encounters and meetings with ordinary people who speak from that wise and intuitive place, the human heart.

On the next pages, you will find a list of some of the authors, poets, spiritual teachers and teachings that have been particularly significant and helpful to me for my spiritual growth and deeper understanding of life. Many of them have accompanied me from the start and I return to them over and over again for further guidance or solace, to re-discover the wisdoms contained in them, and receive a helping hand when I need to re-orientate or find my bearings.

This is by no means an exhaustive list, but will hopefully serve you as pointer to potential sources for further exploration and inquiry into who you are and what this life as a human being is all about.

For ease of reference, I have simply listed them in alphabetical order.

Name	**Books / Videos /Podcasts / Courses / Retreats.**
A.I.M (Associazione Italiana per la Mindfulness)	Course: MBSR (Mindulness-Based Stress Reduction), led by Fabio Giommi and Antonella Commellato, Milan, Italy.
Isabel Allende	Books: The House of Spirits; Paula; Eva Luna; The Faithful Gardener.
Rick Archer	Video: Buddha at the Gas Pump. www.batgap.com
Coleman Barks	Books: A Year with Rumi; The Essential Rumi; Rumi: The Book of Love.

Sondra Barrett	Book: Secrets of Your Cells: Awakening the Body's Inner Intelligence
Melissa Blacker	Book: The Book of Mu; Recordings: Dharma talks & teachings, Boundless Way Zen, MA, USA.
Jean Shinoda Bolen	Books: The Tao of Psychology; Urgent Message from Mother.
Boundless Way Zen	Retreats: Sesshin & Mindfulness led by Melissa Blacker & David Rynick in Italy, UK and USA.
Gregory Boyle	Book: Tattoos on the Heart: The Power of Boundless Compassion.
Tara Brach	Video: Tara Talks: Tarabrach.com. Books: Self-Acceptance; True Refuge.
Julia Cameron	Course: The Artist's Way. Books: The Right to Write; The Well of Creativity.
Joseph Campbell	Book: The Hero with a Thousand Faces.
Pema Chödrön	Books: Getting Unstuck; When Things Fall Apart; Walking the Walk; Welcoming the Unwelcome.
Paulo Coehlo	Books: The Alchemist; By the River Piedra, I Sat Down and Wept.
Dalai Lama, Desmond Tutu	Book: The Book of Joy
Anthony De Mello	Books: Awareness; Wellsprings; Taking Flight.
Donna Eden	Books: Eden Energy Medicine; Foundation Training in EEM.
Clarissa Pinkola Estès	Books: Women who run with the Wolves; The Faithful Gardener.
Kalhil Gibran	Book: The Prophet
Gangaji	Books: Diamond in Your Pocket; Hidden Treasure. Podcasts: Being Yourself – Self Inquiry with Gangaji and Conversations with Gangaji – www.gangaji.org;

S.N. Goenka	Course: Vipassana meditation (training and volunteering), Florence, Italy.
Natalie Goldberg	Books: Writing Down the Bones; Long Quiet Highway; (et al) The Well of Creativity.
Joseph Goldstein	Book: Abiding in Mindfulness.
Tich Nhat Hanh	Books: Mindful Living; Peace; Call me by my True Names. Retreat: spring retreat at Plum Village, France.
John Hill	Book: At Home in the World: Sounds and Symmetries of Belonging.
ISAP	Conference & retreat: Jungian Odyssey Series - the Playful Psyche by ISAP, International School for Analytical Psychology, Zurich, CH.
C.G. Jung	Books: Memories, Dreams, Reflections; Man and his Symbols; The Symbolic Life (Vol.18, The Collected Works).
C.G. Jung Institute	Course: Intensive Study Program, Zurich, CH. www.junginstitut.ch
Anodea Judith	Books: Wheels of Life; Eastern body, Western Mind.
Jon Kabat-Zinn	Books: Wherever you go, There you are; Coming to our Senses; Full Catastrophe Living.
Matt Kahn	Book: Whatever Arises, Love That. Videos: Matt Kahn All For Love.
Byron Katie	Book: Loving What is. Course: The Work.
Madison King	Course: Foundation Training in Eden Energy Medicine, UK.
J. Krishnamurti	Book: Freedom from the Known
Linda Schierse Leonard	Books: Meeting the Madwoman; The Call to Create.
Anne Morrow Lindbergh	Book: Gift from the Sea

Tim Macartney	Book: Finding Earth Finding Soul.
Dawna Markova	Book: I Will Not Die an Unlived Life.
Fleet Maull	Book: Radical Responsibility.
Alice Miller	Book: The Drama of Being a Child.
Oriah Mountain Dreamer	Book: The Invitation
Kristin Neff	Course: Self Compassion Step by Step. Book: Self Compassion: Stop Beating Yourself Up and Leave Insecurity Behind.
Mark Nepo	Books: Holding Nothing Back; Seven Thousand Ways to Listen; The Way Under the Way.
John O'Donohue	Books: Longing and Belonging; Beauty; Anam Cara: A Book of Celtic Wisdom.
Sharon Olds	Book: Odes
Mary Oliver	Books: A Poetry Handbook; Why I Wake Early; A Thousand Mornings: Poems.
On Being Project	Podcast: www.onbeing.org – Krista Tippet's public radio & podcast on the art of living.
Pádraig Ó Tuama	Video: Imagining Peace TEDx talk 2016; Podcast: Poetry Unbound, On Being
Parker J. Palmer	Book: Let Your Life Speak.
Rainer Maria Rilke	Book: Sonnets to Orpheus with Letters to a Young Poet.
Sir Ken Robinson	Books: The Element; Out of Our Minds.
Lorin Roche	Book: The Radiance Sutras: 112 Gateways to the Yoga of Wonder and Delight.
Don Miguel Ruiz	Books: The Four Agreements; Beyond Fear.
David Rynick	Book: This Truth Never Fails, also Life Coaching and Dharma talks, Boundless Way Zen Temple, MA, USA.

ShantiMayi	Book: In Our Hearts We Know.
Tami Simon	Book: Being True: What Matters Most in Work, Life and Love.
Sounds True	Podcast: Insights at the Edge: Weekly Wisdom by founder, Tami Simon on SoundsTrue.com.
William Stafford	Books: Crossing Unmarked Snow; Writing the Australian Crawl.
Shunryu Suzuki	Book: Zen Mind, Beginner's Mind.
Susan M. Tiberghien	Books: Looking for Gold; Circling to the Center; Footsteps
Bruce Tift	Book: Already Free: Buddhism Meets Psychotherapy on the Path of Liberation.
Krista Tippet	Book: Becoming Wise: An Inquiry into the Mystery and Art of Living. See also OnBeing.
Eckhart Tolle	Books: The Power of Now; A New Earth.
Swami Vidyanand	Course: Yoga teacher training, Sri Ma School of Transformational Hatha Yoga, Pondicherry, India.
Neale Donald Walsch	Books: Conversations with God, books 1-3.
David Whyte	Books: The House of Belonging; Consolations. Audio: What to Remember when Waking; Midlife and the Great Unknown.
Marion Woodman	Book: Addiction to Perfection.
Oprah Winfrey	Video and TV: Super Soul Sunday series.

Books by the Same Author

Marrying it All, Diana F. Button, iUniverse 2003.

A novel set in Luxembourg: in a land where nothing is as it appears and there are no words for the phrase 'I love you,' it is not just the story's heroine Sabina who is whisked away on a journey in which reality and fantasy, past and present, comedy and tragedy become inextricably intertwined; we all are - characters and readers alike. And the answer to the journey's question is both a question and an answer: Marrying it all?

Bubbles to the Surface...Liberating words, BoD, 2011.

Poetry - a collection of short poems, or 'bubbles' that come into being through creative play with words and bubble to the surface of consciousness and out into the world. Out of print

Second edition planned, spring 2020.

Other Publications planned for 2020 and beyond:

Lighting Up My House
Non-fiction: a personal story of Jungian philosophy and analysis through dreams and artwork.

Living the Animal
Non-fiction:: animal symbology in personal dreams and stories and their meaning for life in this world and the collective psyche.

This is Not About Poems
A collection of around 50 poems that explore layers of meaning and metaphor.